The Trump revolt

Manchester University Press

POCKET POLITICS
SERIES EDITOR: BILL JONES

Pocket politics presents short, pithy summaries of complex topics on socio-political issues both in Britain and overseas. Academically sound, accessible and aimed at the interested general reader, the series will address a subject range including political ideas, economics, society, the machinery of government and international issues. Unusually, perhaps, authors are encouraged, should they choose, to offer their own conclusions rather than strive for mere academic objectivity. The series will provide stimulating intellectual access to the problems of the modern world in a user-friendly format.

Previously published
Reform of the House of Lords   Philip Norton

The Trump revolt

Edward Ashbee

Manchester University Press

Copyright © Edward Ashbee 2017

The right of Edward Ashbee to be identified as the author of this work has been asserted by him in accordance with the Copyright, Designs and Patents Act 1988

Published by Manchester University Press
Altrincham Street, Manchester M1 7JA

www.manchesteruniversitypress.co.uk

British Library Cataloguing-in-Publication Data
A catalogue record for this book is available from the British Library

ISBN   978 1 5261 2298 8   paperback

First published 2017

The publisher has no responsibility for the persistence or accuracy of URLs for any external or third-party internet websites referred to in this book, and does not guarantee that any content on such websites is, or will remain, accurate or appropriate

Typeset
by Toppan Best-set Premedia Limited

Contents

Acknowledgements		*page* vi
1	Introduction	1
2	The populist tradition and the American state	8
3	'Trumpism'	22
4	Voters	61
5	Sequences	80
6	Order, timing and chance	85
7	Afterword: Donald Trump, neoliberalism and political reconfiguration	88
References		96
Index		113

Acknowledgements

I am very grateful indeed to John L. Campbell (Dartmouth College), Joachim Lund, Morten Ougaard, Len Seabrooke (Department of Business and Politics, Copenhagen Business School) and John Dumbrell as well as seminar participants in both Denmark and the UK for their helpful comments about early drafts of the book. It goes without saying that I am alone responsible for errors or omissions.

something will crack. The non-suburban electorate will decide that the system has failed and start looking around for a strongman to vote for – someone willing to assure them that, once he is elected, the smug bureaucrats, tricky lawyers, overpaid bond salesmen, and postmodernist professors will no longer be calling the shots. (Richard Rorty, 1998: 90)

1

Introduction

> It is the end of an era ... that of neoliberalism ... It remains to be seen what will succeed it ... After Brexit and this election, everything is now possible. A world is collapsing before our eyes. (Gérard Araud, French Ambassador to the US, November 8th 2016 (quoted in Borger, 2016))

WHEN Donald Trump stepped onto the stage to claim victory at the New York Hilton Midtown he seemed unusually subdued. This was perhaps fitting. Just a few hours earlier, Trump had been said to have no mathematical possibility of securing victory. Nonetheless, although he eventually came up well short in terms of winning the popular vote and his margins in some states were wafer-thin, his predicted Electoral College Vote was decisive.[1] There was also some evidence of a 'coattails' effect insofar as Trump's victory may have helped the Republicans in down-ballot races. Certainly, once all the votes had been counted, the Republicans controlled the White House, Congress, 33 governorships and both chambers of 32 state legislatures. As Nile Gardiner of the Heritage Foundation remarked: 'Never since the Twenties have the Republicans wielded such influence' (Gardiner, 2016). The result defied the expectations of almost all pollsters and pundits as well as the campaign teams.

Despite the different October and November surprises that her campaign had faced, most notably the FBI Director's decision to reopen inquiries into her emails, almost all the usual indicators in the run-up to Election Day had suggested a broad, albeit shallow, lead for Clinton. It was assumed that even if she failed to win in swing states such as Florida and North Carolina or take target states such as Arizona, she had a 'firewall' of solidly Democratic North-Eastern and Upper-Midwest states that would assure an Electoral College majority. Yet, after just a few hours of vote counting it was more than clear that the 'firewall' had collapsed and Trump had by then not one but a number of routes to the 270 Electoral Votes required to secure the presidency.[2] From then on, it was easy. Trump's victory was, according to Paul Ryan, the Speaker of the US House of Representatives who had distanced himself from Trump during much of the campaign, 'the most incredible political feat' that he had seen in his lifetime (Bruce, Siegel and Parkinson, 2016).

Ryan was not exaggerating. When Trump first launched his presidential bid in mid-June 2015 at Trump Tower, Nate Silver, the doyen of American polling analysts, put his chances of winning the Republican nomination, much less the presidency itself, at just 2 per cent. Trump would, it was said, like other fringe candidates such as Herman Cain, or Michele Bachmann who gained short-lived flurries of support in earlier contests, quickly crash and burn. Such candidacies, Silver asserted, go through different stages of doom. There would be heightened scrutiny that would expose personal and political liabilities. Then, even if Trump survived the early caucuses and primaries, he 'would soon be bypassed as the rest of the field consolidated down to one or two other establishment-backed alternatives' (Silver, 2015).

Those who, like Silver, derided Trump's prospects could also draw upon scholarly heavyweights. In particular, they could cite the 2008 study, *The Party Decides*, which made the claim that that despite the excitement often generated by the early primaries and caucuses and talk in recent battles of grassroots activists becoming pivotal in shaping the parties' futures, the eventual nominee is in effect chosen by the interests that collectively constitute the party (Cohen, Karol, Noel and Zaller, 2009). The period before the primaries begin (sometimes dubbed the 'invisible primary'), within which candidates first put themselves forward, jostle for position, assemble teams and secure support from within the party 'establishment', is thus pivotal.

From this perspective, the eventual 2016 Republican nominee would be someone such as former Florida Governor Jeb Bush, Senator Marco Rubio or Governor John Kasich, just as other figures with elite backing, for example Mitt Romney who had won the primary battle in 2012 and Senator John McCain who had been chosen in 2008, had proved victorious. The consensus was that while a more radical figure, perhaps drawn from the ranks of the Tea Party movement would almost certainly make a stand in 2016, he or she would eventually be cast aside as elite interests used their resources to ensure that their anointed candidate was victorious.

None of this was, of course, to be. Despite their spending power, the party 'establishment' candidates were swept aside. Bush, Kasich and Rubio crashed and burned. Texas Senator Ted Cruz, who had long been seen as an ideological zealot and outcast by many fellow Republicans in Congress was the last man standing in the battle to deny Trump the nomination and he thus gained a measure of rather reluctant elite backing as the only credible alternative. Nonetheless, even Cruz succumbed following his defeat in the Indiana primary.

Following the conclusion of the nomination fight, there had then been widespread expectations that Trump would 'pivot', embrace conventional political norms and direct his campaign towards the median voter. That had, after all, been with just a few exceptions, the conventional route to the presidency although the claims and commitments that candidates felt compelled to give during the primaries sometimes limited their ability to secure middle-ground votes at a later stage.

Trump, however, stubbornly failed to pivot. His vituperative early morning tweets and verbal assaults continued. He faced numerous accusations about his personal conduct that led many within his own party's ranks to condemn him. Instead of moving towards less abrasive positions and classical political formulae the populist streak that had always defined his campaign became even more pronounced as the US moved towards Election Day. On many issues it constituted a sharp break with the mix of economic and cultural policies that had defined Republican Party politics since the 1970s although there had been some hints of what was to come in both the 2008 and 2012 contests. Angry crowds at Trump rallies not only demanded the building of a border wall and imprisonment of Hillary Clinton but also cheered demands to 'drain the Washington swamp'. A final campaign advertisement appeared to draw upon 'Alt-Right' thinking (see pp. 47–52) lambasting Wall Street and globalism in terms that, paradoxically, resembled the critiques put forward by the further reaches of the left:

> The establishment has trillions of dollars at stake in this election. For those who control the levers of power in Washington, and for the global special interests, they partner with these people that don't have your good in mind. (quoted in Jennifer Williams, 2016)

Commentators were dismissive. Although it was acknowledged that this strategy could win loyal and enthusiastic backing amongst some voters (those whom Hillary Clinton was to dub 'deplorables'), it was seen as too narrow a slice of the electorate. Thus, Trump's defeat seemed assured. To many he appeared such an improbable figure.

Inevitably, therefore, even before the final votes were tallied on November 8th, searching and sometimes wracked questions began to be thrown around. They were all variations on a single theme. How did a candidate who broke with almost every single norm governing candidate behaviour, appeared to eschew the professionalised forms of campaigning that have been adopted in recent years, and who had been more or less disowned by Republican elites, prove victorious?

This book seeks to answer that question. It argues that the Trump campaign, like earlier populist insurgencies, can be explained in part by considering some defining features of US political culture and, in particular, attitudes towards government. Having said that, 'culture' is a term that must, however, be employed with very considerable caution. It is all too easy to draw upon unsubstantiated cultural generalisations that edge towards crude stereotypes. Furthermore, in many accounts, 'culture' is the end of the story in presenting explanations of political processes. For example, the importance attached to 'gun rights' or to opposition to healthcare reform is often explained away with a simple reference to long-held beliefs and values. In contrast, while this book considers political culture, it does not present it as an independent variable or 'free-floating'. Instead, as Chapter 2 suggests, attitudes towards government and popular sentiments about the legitimate role of government have in large part been shaped and moulded by the defining institutional characteristics of the American state. Those characteristics contribute to shaping the content of political debate and setting the terms on which ideas may either come to the fore or alternatively fall by the wayside. Nonetheless, while those characteristics, and the components of US political culture that have been shaped by them, are important in terms of explaining the background to Trump's victory they are a necessary but not sufficient condition. If we look beyond cultural factors, the book argues that in overall terms, several factors were of particular importance during election year. They are a mix of both ideational and 'material' processes. First, although some commentators might be reluctant to admit it, the strategic and entrepreneurial skills of Trump campaign (and as a corollary the failings of the Clinton campaign), should be considered. In many respects, Trump was a particularly effective and successful ideational entrepreneur. A second important factor lies in the composition of the different voting blocs. The financial crisis of 2008–2009 and the economic malaise that followed in its wake accelerated shifts, in particular long-running realignment processes, that allowed Trump to win narrow victories in some all-important 'Rust Belt' states. Other factors also contributed to Trump's victory. The election outcome can be seen as the end result of what might be termed *reactive sequences* set in motion by the processes of intense partisan polarisation that defined American politics over preceding decades and the electoral strategies pursued by Republican elites. They set off a series of chain reactions. The book argues furthermore that another factor, which is not usually included in discussions of electoral politics, should be brought into the picture. Any explanation of the final outcome also has to incorporate the timing of particular developments, the order in which they took place and of course simple chance events.

This book argues that each of these overlapping factors contributed to both Trump's victories on the path to the Republican nomination and his eventual capture of the presidency. On top of this, other questions should however be addressed. Does the election have broader implications? Does Trump's victory signal, as the French Ambassador to the US asserted, the demise of neoliberalism? Or, to ask a perhaps more limited question, did the election usher in a process of reconfiguration that is changing the political bases upon which neoliberalism has hitherto been structured? Are old and once familiar political cleavages now being displaced by new forms of division? And, furthermore, is all of this a story of American exceptionalism? Or should we instead focus on the many similarities and overlaps between the Trump campaign and the right-wing populist parties in Europe? Is *il*liberalism spreading as part of a process of change taking place across much of the developed world? The Afterword considers this.

Four further points should be added about the book. First, there are inevitably extensive overlaps and crossovers between the different chapters. Ideas and 'material' processes always interact. Much will be said about voters during the discussion about the Trump campaign's ideas. Similarly, the survey of the Trump electorate also considers the ideas that motivated these voters. Second, although much of the book surveys the ideas, processes and shifts that contributed to Trump's eventual victory, it is not seeking to provide a comprehensive account of the election. Relatively little is thus said about the other contenders for the Republican presidential nomination, the character of the Clinton campaign, or issues that may have contributed to her defeat such as the apparent hacking and leaking of emails. All of that is addressed in many other studies. The focus of this book is on Trump and his campaign. Third, all accounts require a cut-off point. This account does not go beyond the November election and its immediate aftermath. Others will track the character of the transition and Trump's assumption of the presidency. Fourth, although they can certainly create a tone or set off chains of reactive sequences, it should be noted that the ideas and pledges that steer campaigns and perhaps contribute to election outcomes are not necessarily a guide to the policies that will be adopted by an incoming administration. Indeed, history suggests that election discourses often provide a very poor guide indeed. Even in periods of unified government when the same party controls the executive and legislative branches, presidents not only face the checks and balances that define the US system of government but there are also processes of path dependence that limit and circumscribe their capacity to bring forth radical forms of change (Ashbee and Dumbrell, 2016: 9–19). Furthermore, Trump will at every point be compelled to negotiate a path with Republican elites that were far distanced from him politically and personally during the 2016 campaign. On top of this, unanticipated events, developments and processes always take their toll on the most developed of plans.

Notes

1 When the Electoral College Vote was formally recorded, the result was – because there were seven 'faithless Electors' – 304 to 227. It should be noted that although the College result was decisive, it was not in historical terms a particularly striking victory. According to *The New York Times* there were 45 presidential elections in which the winning candidate had won a larger share of the Electoral Vote (Patel and Andrews, 2016). Hillary Clinton won just over 51 per cent of the two-party popular vote.

2 Paradoxically the authors of the US Constitution had regarded the Electoral College as a check on the popular vote that would prevent those who were ill-prepared or unqualified securing the presidency. For Alexander Hamilton, 'the office of President will never fall to the lot of any man who is not in an eminent degree endowed with the requisite qualifications' (Hamilton, n.d.).

2

The populist tradition and the American state

POPULISM has a particular place within the US political tradition. In the post-war period alone, there have been recurrent right-wing populist insurgencies. In the 1950s, McCarthyism went well beyond anti-communism, lambasted the East Coast elites, and drew upon fears of modernity, cosmopolitanism and non-conformity. In the 1960s and 1970s, Alabama Governor George Wallace not only proclaimed 'segregation now, segregation tomorrow, segregation forever', but in his presidential bids made a pitch for white working votes in both the South and North by drawing upon the legacy of the New Deal. In the 1990s Patrick J. Buchanan contested the Republican primaries by appealing to white 'middle American radicals' by attacking immigration and free trade.[1] Although closer to core Republican traditions, the Tea Party movement which took shape in early 2009 just a few weeks after President Obama's inauguration, also drew upon quasi-populist visions of a struggle by the citizenry to restore constitutional government.

Although there were important differences, the 2016 Trump campaign reproduced some of the ideas and frames that defined these earlier movements and was thereby tied to a long tradition. As will be seen in later chapters of the book, that tradition interweaves nationalism together with vituperative hostility towards the established 'political class' and governing institutions, particularly those at federal level.

Why do such sentiments have a hold? Some accounts point to the creative efforts of well-placed ideational entrepreneurs and the efforts of conservative networks that have in some circumstances embraced populist messages. Skilled campaigners can, it is said, mould and mobilise mass opinion, at times playing upon the endemic racial and ethnic fractures that have defined the American experience. The absence of a mass socialist or social democratic party may also have played a role insofar as it allowed populism to claim the mantle of anti-elitist politics that the left might otherwise have grasped.

Others attribute anti-government attitudes on which Trump capitalised to the seemingly exceptional nature of US political culture citing, for example, the 'frontier' thesis. This rests on Frederick Jackson Turner's celebrated 1893 claim that American identity was shaped by the rugged individualism of life on the frontier between European settlement and the untamed wilderness beyond. This gave rise to a suspicion of, and impatience with, the machinery of government and the formal procedures associated with it. Although the frontier thesis's inherent monocausality and the way in which it neglects the place of other cultural inheritances in the making of the US have been fiercely challenged, it remains as a point of reference.

There are alternative approaches. It could be argued that it would be a mistake to explain the Trump campaign or other outbursts of right-wing populism in the US by considering American history alone. After all, populist sentiments have a comparable place in many European countries. For example, as polls conducted in the second half of 2016 suggested, attitudes towards immigration, Islam and 'political correctness' were very similar in the US and Denmark (although, having said that, only 4 per cent of Danes admitted to supporting Trump's presidential campaign) (Motta, 2016). Nonetheless, although there were movements such as *Poujadisme* in 1950s France, European right-wing populism has for the most part more recent origins. The growth of populist sentiment is closely tied to globalising processes, the decline of the traditional parties, immigration and the development of European Union as an economic and political project.

In contrast, in the US, right-wing populism has been a recurrent and ingrained feature of the political process over a long period. And, although the values and beliefs derived from the country's political culture and the activities of particular ideational 'entrepreneurs' should not be discounted when seeking to explain this, some features of the twentieth-century American experience make up an important part of the story. In particular, the structural characteristics of the contemporary American state, and the ways in which these are perceived and understood by large numbers of people, particularly within the white population, add to and build upon long-held resentments about the legitimate place and efficacy of government.[2] While such structural characteristics cannot in themselves explain why the Trump campaign took off and gained traction at specific points in 2015–2016 they do explain why right-wing populism has been a significant and enduring feature of twentieth- and twenty-first century US politics and why, in certain settings and circumstances such as those that opened up in 2015–2016, populist attitudes can come to the forefront of politics.

Five structural characteristics of the American state appear to be of particular significance in the shaping of attitudes. First, large parts of the state are, to appropriate Suzanne Mettler's term, 'submerged'. In place of direct provision by departments and agencies they instead rest upon a mass of federal government policies that provide incentives (or disincentives) for particular private sector actors. In particular, tax concessions are widely used to subsidise particular activities, many of which offer direct benefits to the middle class (Mettler, 2011). For example, there are tax exemptions on health insurance cover and retirement savings as well as the home mortgage interest deduction. Despite their size and scale they are largely invisible to their recipients because such tax credits are far less evident to the recipient than an expenditure programme and, relatedly, because there is no direct physical contact with a government official (King, 2016: 296). As Mettler notes, 'the submerged state simultaneously eludes most ordinary citizens: they have little awareness of its policies or their upwardly redistributive effects' (Mettler, 2010: 803). Christopher Howard argues along similar lines in his studies of tax arrangements and points to what he terms the 'hidden welfare state' or 'the welfare state nobody knows', suggesting that in terms of size, scope and functions it is comparable with formal, recognised and established social programmes such as Social Security (Howard, 1997; Howard, 2007):

> In short, the American welfare state may be unusual, but less for its small size than for its reliance on a wide variety of policy tools to achieve what many European welfare states do primarily through social insurance ... we should be highly suspicious of anyone who declares that the United States has a small welfare state. (Howard, 2007: 19)

Howard's claim about the scale of provision was vividly illustrated by a McKinsey Global Institute report considering real incomes between 2005 and 2014. US government transfers turned a four-point decline in median market income into a one percentage point gain in 'take home' disposable income (compared with a net change of just 3 per cent in France) (Dobbs, Madgavkar, Woetzel, Bughin, Labaye and Kashyap, 2016: 14).

The scale of these programmes is such that they have a profound impact on US society and the economy through their scale, the consequences that they have upon individual lives, the interests that they create or bolster, the delegation of authority to non-state 'private' actors, the further blurring of an already imprecise line between the state and civil society and the political dynamics that they set in motion. Furthermore, many of these programmes command widespread support. And yet, given their 'submerged' or 'hidden' character, government (particularly the federal government) does not secure political credit or kudos for them.

Some other programmes have a degree of visibility, but are not perceived as government provision or regarded as being at arms-length from government. Fannie Mae (The Federal National Mortgage Association) and Freddie Mac (The Federal Home Loan Mortgage Corporation) structured the character of the housing market over many decades but were seen by individuals and the markets as distanced from government policymakers. There is still a widespread belief, for example, that because benefits or 'entitlement' programmes such as Social Security, Medicare and Medicare Part D are based in part upon earlier contributions, they therefore have little to do with government as such. They appear to be seen as a public version of private insurance. This was highlighted in the widely reported demand raised by a Tea Party supporting attendee at a town hall meeting convened at the peak of the movement's campaigning. He is said to have told his member of Congress in Simpsonville, South Carolina, to 'keep your government hands off my Medicare' (quoted in Rucker, 2009). In sum, and in contrast with some European countries particularly the Scandinavian nations, the US state is rarely acknowledged as a social provider.

There are different but interrelated reasons why American state provision developed in this way. The absence of a credible social democratic tradition that might have pulled the US towards more overt state interventionism was a factor. Often, indirect expenditure through the tax regime was a means by which political actors could avoid the political opprobrium and scrutiny that is tied to the creation of new agencies and departments or the introduction of new large-scale spending programmes. The use of 'tax expenditures' and subsidies disarmed those who might otherwise have lobbied against a particular form of social assistance and as both housing and healthcare provision developed, established interests were in effect 'bought off' through subsidies and incentives. This has been termed 'passive intervention' and was characteristic of periods when there was 'enough support to get social programs passed but not enough to challenge established interests' (Starr and Esping-Andersen, 1979: 15).

The American state has a second defining feature. Alongside the laws, programmes and policies that collectively constitute the 'hidden' or 'submerged' state, some other institutions within the American state have a strikingly, often intrusively, visible character. In many instances, they are deeply unpopular, particularly amongst those who vote Republican or say that they 'lean' towards the Republicans. They include the Department of Health and Human

Services, the Environmental Protection Agency, the Department of Education, and the Internal Revenue Service (Pew Research Center, 2015a: 61).

Why are these agencies and departments the target of opprobrium? In part, it is because there are issues of bureaucratic complexity that do much to confirm the popular belief that the machinery of government is inherently inefficient. Often the relationships between federal and state governments are not based upon complementarities but instead marked by tension and conflict. Just at a federal level, departments, agencies, bureaux and commissions jostle with each other. There are overlapping and interlocking jurisdictions that hamper programme administration and accountability (Jacobs and King, 2009: 11). Agencies are torn between loyalty to both the administration and Congress. Each agency has its own working cultures and often, in search of reputational enhancement, it will have a competitive relationship with other sections of the government. Compared with private sector firms, low pay rates (if related to qualifications) and the value of skills that public officials possess have led to relatively high rates of turnover and low institutional memory within government agencies (Carpenter, 2005: 59). Furthermore, political appointees who have overall responsibility for departments and agencies may well owe their jobs to loyalty rather than professional skills or expertise. All this can contribute to a marked institutional sluggishness particularly at times of crisis.

Government, or at least its visible components, is also unpopular because of its perceived impact. The Internal Revenue Service (IRS) has been the object of particular criticism. Tax authorities are invariably and inevitably regarded with suspicion and sometimes seen as favouring particular groupings while victimising others. Nonetheless, in the case of the IRS and the US tax regime, there are particular reasons for that hostility amongst those in some middle and higher income bands. First, there is no national sales tax, which is in European countries hidden in the total price paid for goods and services, and therefore the federal government is largely dependent upon income tax which has a much more visible character.

Furthermore, the overall US tax regime is in relative terms rather more progressive than commentators often assume. Indeed, if social insurance is taken together with income taxes, the result is heavily progressive, thus laying a basis for resentments amongst those in middle and higher income groupings. It results in an average combined marginal rate of 7.7 per cent for those earning under $10,000 annually and 44.6 per cent for those who make over a million dollars (Lundeen, 2015). The US regime is, at least in part, relatively progressive in character because there are high indirect tax rates in much of Europe, particularly the Nordic countries. These sales taxes are heavily regressive in character and inevitably impose a significant burden on those placed on the lower rungs of the economic ladder. By depending upon income taxes to a greater extent, and providing negative tax credits, US taxation takes a proportionately higher toll on those occupying the middle and higher rungs of the ladder. Redistribution takes place in Europe *within* classes (or across phases of an individual's life given high personal insurance contributions) whereas it takes place to a greater extent in the US *between* classes (Prasad, 2006: 25).[3] All this has political consequences:

> regressive taxation keeps the wealthy on the side of the welfare state in Europe, allowing a kind of redistribution that is politically tolerated by all classes, namely, within-class redistribution. Meanwhile, progressive taxation consigns the US to frequent conflict over revenue generation. (Prasad and Deng, 2009: 432)[4]

Similarly, there are also important differences between the US and Europe if the character and overall impact of social or welfare provision is considered. As has been widely noted, and although its extent can be exaggerated, the principle of universalism has more of a hold in Europe. Thus, services or assistance are provided for all more or less regardless of income. The take-up of such services is, however, unequal. If considered on a per capita basis, some benefits including higher education and healthcare provision give much, and perhaps disproportionately more, to those in the middle and higher-income groupings than to those with lower incomes if only because the former make more intensive use of that provision. This may do much to explain why, four decades after the neoliberal revolution began, some forms of social provision still enjoy widespread legitimacy and support in Europe. Because there is cross-class usage, they have captured cross-class support.

In the US, however, and this also has important implications, benefits are more narrowly targeted and generally take a 'residual' form. Although the means testing that residual programmes necessitate often takes what is seen as an oppressive and intrusive form, such programmes are more openly redistributive in character. Because they are redistributive and offer little or nothing to those further up the ladder and are in some cases given to those often seen as undeserving, they command much less support than the social programmes in Europe. There is less cross-class backing and therefore such programmes become an open and easy target for populist anger. Thus, as has been seen, the Trump campaign promised to protect 'entitlements' such as Medicare and Social Security (that are in part based upon contributions) but offered no such guarantees to the recipients of 'residual' programmes such as Medicaid.

Because many programmes have a residual character, the assistance they provide provokes particular anger amongst the groupings that miss out because of inevitable design flaws. These are the groups that are placed just above the maximum limit for certain benefits or forms of assistance. In an unguarded aside during the 2016 presidential election campaign, former President Bill Clinton called the Patient Protection and Affordable Care Act (Obamacare) 'the craziest thing in the world' because it placed significant numbers in a position whereby they earned too much to be given federal insurance subsidies but faced steeply rising health insurance premiums (Berman, 2016). Those placed in that position have every reason to resent those who have a slightly lower income level and are thus eligible for assistance.

Just as the tax regime is seen to penalise middle-income groupings, the regulatory regime is, if federal and state government measures are taken together, more far-reaching and rule-based in character than those who instinctively think of the US in terms of 'limited government'. In 1986, David Vogel concluded that US industry 'has been forced to struggle harder to resist additional government restrictions on its prerogatives than in any other capitalist nation' (Vogel, 1986: 28). Although there are questions about the effectiveness of regulations that are imposed and the extent to which they are enforced, the US regulatory process had, furthermore, rather more stakeholders ('nonindustry constituencies') thereby limiting, still further, a particular firm's room for manoeuvre (Vogel, 1986: 146). There is little reason to revisit or revise this conclusion. Anecdotal evidence invariably suggests that European exporters are far more fearful of regulatory authorities in the US than those in the European Union.

Furthermore, US regulatory provisions have become broader and deeper in recent years. Given its inability to pursue a legislative strategy because of the Republicans' hold over Congress, and so as to keep pace with industrial change, the Obama administration used the regulatory capacity of the executive branch to the full. Estimates published in August 2016 suggested that the administration had issued 641 major rules during the Obama years (compared with 426 during George W. Bush's terms of office). The cost was put at $743 billion (Devaney, 2016).

There are thus solid 'material' reasons why there are highly negative perceptions of regulations and the regulatory process in the US. According to Pew polling, 51 per cent of respondents believe that government regulation of business 'usually does more harm than good' while only 44 per cent say that regulation 'is necessary to protect the public interest'. Having said this, the educational divide considered in Chapter 4 again plays an important part in shaping opinion and views are differentiated on the basis of educational attainment levels. Some 59 per cent of those with graduate qualifications believe that regulation is necessary while those who have not been to college see it very differently (just 34 per cent regard regulation as necessary). In the 2016 election, there were, inevitably, strikingly different opinions about regulatory processes between Trump and Clinton supporters (Pew Research Center, 2016b).

Third, the character of the American state is such that it creates a very strong sense of 'winning' or 'losing'. Systems of government resting upon an executive presidency (where there can by definition be only one winner) particularly when combined with a legislative branch elected on the basis of a simple plurality, necessarily create feelings of victory or defeat. There are of course winners and losers in all political systems but that reality is ameliorated in proportional parliamentary systems where governing parties are compelled to reach across the aisle to pass significant parts of their legislative programme. In the US, the sense of 'winner takes all' is reinforced by the 'spoils system', through which an incoming president makes, subject in most cases to the advice and consent of the Senate, 4,000 or so political appointments in both the White House and across the higher reaches of the federal government bureaucracy. It is worth adding to this that the US system of government gives rise to feelings of loss much more often than a sense of winning. Even if a party holds the White House and Congress, outright victories are very rare when there are extensive checks and balances. The passage of legislation requires 60 votes, a super-majority, in the Senate. Certainly, very large majorities of both conservative Republicans (81 per cent) and moderate and liberal Republicans (75 per cent) have told pollsters that their political side loses more often than it wins (Pew Research Center, 2015b: 10). Thus, the right felt that they were invariably the 'losers' during the Obama years despite the Republicans' hold over Congress.

Some of the major policy reforms enacted early in the Obama era added to the sense that some had won while others, particularly the white middle class, had lost out badly. In particular, the Homeowners Affordability and Stability Plan that sought to protect households from foreclosure, the American Recovery and Reinvestment Act (ARRA) which provided a substantial fiscal stimulus as the 'Great Recession' took hold, and the Patient Protection and Affordable Care Act which established 'Obamacare', created feelings amongst some that were losers. Although ARRA incorporated tax concessions intended to secure Republican support, they were largely invisible to the recipients. And, the spending components of the Act appeared to offer benefits to those at the lowest end of the scale and 'the undeserving' rather than middle America. The televised comments by Rick Santelli, a commentator, on CNBC about the Stability Plan are regarded as the starting point for the Tea Party movement. They capture the redistributive fears that underpinned the Tea Party movement's radicalism and the Trump campaign:

> How many of you people want to pay for your neighbor's mortgage who has an extra bathroom and can't pay their bills? ... President Obama, are you listening? ... We're thinking about having a Chicago tea party in July. All of you capitalists that want to show up to Lake Michigan, I'm going to start organizing it. (quoted in McCain, 2009)

The Affordable Care Act also played a part in creating fears and a sense of potential loss. There were not only fears amongst the middle class about the rising cost of insurance premiums but also amongst senior citizens who believed that health facilities, including family doctors, would be placed under greater pressure and overstretched if insurance cover was extended. This was compounded by a sense that those who were newly covered were less deserving. There were parallel concerns that Obamacare would in part be funded by reductions in the growth of Medicare spending (Judis, 2016: 55).

Fourth, as has been widely noted in accounts of the US political process, the character of the Constitution and the place assigned by it to the federal courts, means that some critical issues that in many other countries are resolved by elected legislatures are decided upon in the US by an unelected judiciary. There is thus a private enforcement regime or what has been dubbed the 'litigation state' (Farhang, 2010). This is in part because of deliberate processes. Where, for example, there were far-reaching differences within Congress or between Congress and the executive branch, or Congress did not want the executive branch to have an adjudicative role, legislators left disputed questions unresolved: 'The legislative choice of private litigation over administrative power emerged from conflict between ideologically antagonistic interests, channelled through America's fragmented political institutions, particularly the dynamic of legislative–executive competition for control of the bureaucracy' (Farhang, 2010: 5). Thus, although some significant reforms such as the National Labor Relations Act of 1935 and the Occupational Safety and Health Act of 1970 did not permit private enforcement lawsuits, other laws ensured that the courts took over the role traditionally assigned to the executive branch of government.[5]

Even more importantly, from a political perspective, profoundly divisive questions regarding race relations, abortion, the rights of gays and lesbians and of course the final outcome of the 2000 presidential election have all been determined in the legal rather than the political arena. This has implications for legitimacy and the ways in which the imposition of policies is regarded. The Court's decisions, in June 2015, to uphold the Affordable Care Act and to establish same-sex marriage as a constitutional right were the latest in a long line of such judgements and in its wake, opinions about the Court reached an all-time low. In July 2015, 43 per cent viewed the Court unfavourably. Among Republicans, the figure was 61 per cent (Pew Research Center, 2015b: 58). Thus, policy questions that are settled in many countries remain contested in the US. They feed into discontent and antagonism towards government.

Fifth, and last, the porosity of the US state and the ability of groupings to seek redress in the courts and employ lobbyists to press claims on their behalf adds credence to claims that some 'special interests' can secure favours for themselves and remould the character of particular policy regimes in ways that offer advantages. The corporate tax regime is illustrative of this. It is characterised by 'thousands of exemptions, deductions, credits, minimum taxes, and special rules that litter the tax code. Indeed, these tax expenditures are so significant to the system that they profoundly shape its very structure' (Steinmo, 1989: 482). In many instances, such tax concessions have been secured by particularistic interests through intense and sustained lobbying processes.

The effects can be seen if a comparison is drawn between the US corporate tax *rate* (the combined federal and state tax rate in 2009 was 39.1 per cent, a rate higher than that in almost all other developed countries including France, Germany, Canada and the UK) and corporate tax *revenue* which is, as a proportion of GDP, substantially lower than many other nations (Tax Foundation, 2009). A study for PricewaterhouseCoopers concluded:

> Although the United States has the second highest statutory corporate tax ... U.S. corporate income tax revenue (federal and state) as a percentage of GDP paradoxically is much lower than the OECD average – 2.2 percent in the United States versus an OECD average of 3.4 percent – over the 2000–2005 period. In short ... the United States has the second highest combined statutory corporate tax rate among OECD countries, yet is tied with Hungary in raising the fourth lowest amount of combined corporate income tax revenue relative to GDP in 2004. (Merrill, 2007: 2)

There are therefore good reasons for many to believe that well-positioned interests can 'bend' government policy so as to secure advantages.[6] That perception has increased over time. According to polling data from the Pew Research Center, whereas in 1964 some 64 per cent believed that government was 'run for the benefit of all the people' the figure had by 2015 sunk to just 19 per cent (Pew Research Center, 2015a: 26).

In sum, there are a substantial number of reasons why the defining characteristics of the contemporary American state provoke not only frustration but also anger. Many benefits have a largely invisible character. The more visible components of the state apparatus have an extractive, regulatory or redistributive role and appear to serve those less deserving while seeming to penalise some middle-income groupings. At the same time, particularistic interests can secure significant advantages or 'loopholes' while core decision-making is often the prerogative of the courts rather than those who are directly accountable to the electorate. These features of the American state create a basis for cleavages and tensions, particularly between those belonging to a broadly defined 'middle-class', some elites, and those on the lowest rungs of the economic ladder. They fuel populist rage.

Notes

1   Ross Perot, the Texas billionaire who contested both the 1992 and 1996 presidential elections (and won 19 per cent of the popular vote in 1992), also ran on a broadly populist platform but although hostile to established political elites, protectionist in character and conveying concerns about illegal immigration and sovereignty it did not share the very pronounced nationalism and nativism of the other insurgencies. Nonetheless, there is some evidence that some of those who had backed Perot went on to back the Trump campaign.

2   In this context the 'state' refers to the overall state apparatus at national, state and local level rather than the 50 individual states and their structures of government.

3   Sven Steinmo notes his surprise at finding that the overall burden on both income and capital is heavier in the US than both the UK and Sweden (Steinmo, 1989: 502).

4   The progressivity of the tax regime may contribute to the higher level of opposition amongst middle-income voters to redistribution in the US than other comparable OECD countries. There may, however, also be a racial dimension insofar as the poor may be understood to be drawn disproportionately from minorities (Cramer, 2016: 16–17).

5   Given the costs of litigation and issues of 'standing', court action has, however, been a form of redress open only to limited numbers of plaintiffs.

6   Much the same can be said about regulatory process (see p. 16). Well-positioned firms and sectors can secure 'regulatory relief' from Congress (Vogel, 1986: 167).

3

'Trumpism'

WITHIN the broad context of generalised anti-government ideas and entrenched populist sentiments outlined in Chapter 2, other ideas and frames were brought to the forefront by the Trump campaign during the course of 2015 and 2016.

At first sight, these ideas do not appear to take a structured or coherent form. Indeed, *National Review*, the flagship US conservative magazine, was brutally dismissive at the beginning of election year:

> Trump is a philosophically unmoored political opportunist who would trash the broad conservative ideological consensus within the GOP in favor of a free-floating populism with strong-man overtones. (*National Review*, 2016: 14)

Others went even further and pointed to Trump's many contradictions, non-sequiturs and 'post-truths'. A September 2016 study concluded that only 4 per cent of Trump's statements could be rated as completely 'true' while another 11 per cent could be rated as 'mostly true.' Some 70 per cent of Trump's statements that the site checked were rated as in some way false (Blow, 2016a). There was also the repeated use of hyperbole in ways that defied all established political norms. Trump's comments on Hillary Clinton's immigration policy in October 2016 were fairly representative:

> she wants to let people just pour in. You could have 650 million people pour in and we do nothing about it ... Think of it. That's what could happen. You triple the size of our country in a week. (quoted in Bump, 2016b)

Nonetheless, there is a rationality and order to these seeming irrationalities. The contradictions and inconsistencies may have been an example of 'kettle logic'. This suggests that even if inconsistent and mutually contradictory arguments are put forward, they can provide an effective and credible basis for winning arguments insofar as it takes the audience's acceptance of just one of the many claims so to do. And, of course, different arguments can win across different audiences (Heer, 2016).

Furthermore, many people are 'low engagement' voters insofar as they do not follow the details of policy debate. Given that the likelihood of an individual vote affecting the overall outcome is very small indeed (particularly given the Electoral College system) and perhaps because of a sense of detachment from a seemingly remote political system there is instead a widespread reliance on the loose and informal cues provided by candidates that in effect offer shortcuts to their broader policy attitudes. Thus, while those in the 'educated classes' may have pored over the contradictions and the more striking forms of hyperbole that the Trump campaign used, others did not see these or disregarded them and relied instead on cues alone.[1] Put another way, many of his supporters were well aware that they were hearing untruthful or hyperbolic statements but this did not really matter because they felt that they had finally found, in Trump, someone who was on their side. Such was their loyalty that as reporters noted, those attending rallies echoed his rhetoric using even the same forms of inflexion.

At the same time, the heavily polarised character of the US electorate provided a fertile breeding ground for the most fervent and hyperbolic denunciations of those in the enemy camp. A Public Policy Polling survey conducted in mid-October 2016 asked questions that lay on the edges between politics and psychology. It found that 40 per cent of likely Trump voters, perhaps those influenced by the Protestant evangelical tradition, believed that Hillary Clinton was an 'actual demon' and 84 per cent said she should be in prison (Public Policy Polling, 2016: 2). There were, as a corollary, processes of cognitive dissonance amongst his supporters when it came to Trump himself. The leaking of the

2005 tape showing the Republican candidate making lewd and abusive comments about women had a very limited impact amongst grassroots supporters. According to one poll, 91 per cent of his backers in Ohio and 90 per cent in Pennsylvania said that the contents of the tape had not changed their view of him (Salvanto, 2016). This persisted after the election. In mid-December 2016 it was reported, for example, that 52 per cent of Republicans believed that Trump had won a majority of the popular vote (Oliver and Wood, 2016).

Thus, although certainly 'unmoored' as *National Review* asserted, and also mired in contradictions and hyperbole, the Trump campaign's thinking, the frames around which it mobilised, and the ideas that secured its votes had a degree of order as well as roots and association, all of which bear analysis. This chapter seeks to provide that.

Some historical context is required. American conservatism and the Republican Party were transformed over the four decades that preceded the 2016 election. Whereas many mid-century Republicans had tacitly accepted the New Deal and 'big government' became even bigger during the Nixon presidency (1969–1974), the new right that emerged after Nixon was toppled, challenged its very foundations. Conservatism was transformed in terms of both content and style and there was an increasingly strident commitment to a 'constitutional order' that would rein in government social provision, promote the free market and facilitate *originalist* forms of jurisprudence that would limit the ability of the federal courts to extend regulation and bring about progressive cultural reforms.

The shaping of contemporary conservatism

While Ronald Reagan's presidency (1981–1989) secured much less in terms of policy achievements than new right apparatchiks might have hoped and if the size of government, when measured in terms of its overall spending as a share of GDP, was bigger when he left office than when he entered the White House, his years in office were nonetheless regarded as a lodestar by the conservative movement. Against this, the presidencies of George H.W. Bush and George W. Bush, and even the efforts of more radical conservative reformers who took control of Congress in the 1994 mid-term elections, could only disappoint.

Nonetheless, despite the disappointments, the forms of conservatism pioneered by the new right made headway. Within a relatively short time period, the few remaining centrist voices in the Republican Party were marginalised. While, when seen from the right, it had a patchy record and judgements often depended upon the whims of 'swing' judges in the ideological middle, the US Supreme Court was in the hands of conservative judges. There was also legislative change. Both Reagan and George W. Bush oversaw the passage of tax cuts. Facing Republican demands and electoral pressures, President Bill Clinton felt compelled to sign a bill dramatically reforming and limiting welfare provision for single parents. There were also important state-level reforms including the construction of rigorous and punitive law and order regimes.

Perhaps most importantly, there were processes of *policy drift* which, while formal programmes and structures remained in place, led to significant changes in the character of government provision and the relationship between government and the individual. For example, over a prolonged period, the federal minimum wage failed to keep pace with inflation. As critical commentators noted, the extent of protection that social provision offered for those facing systemic disadvantage (including not only the urban 'underclass' but also sections of the 'middle class') was squeezed, leaving many individuals and households cut adrift:

> Although most U.S. public social programs have indeed resisted radical retrenchment, the American social welfare framework has also, in crucial areas, offered increasingly incomplete protection against the key social risks that Americans confront. (Hacker, 2004: 243)

Nonetheless, despite the Republican policy record, the impact of drift and the institutionalisation of a conservative 'common sense' as the ideational centre of gravity and the overall political agenda moved rightwards, there were serious tensions within the movement and between different Republican constituencies. By the 1990s, US conservatism had come to be structured around three distinct and discernible strands or currents and there were also countless sub-currents. Different labels can be attached to the currents but these were what can be called in very broad terms *economic conservatism, cultural conservatism* and *neo-conservatism*.

Economic conservatism is in ideational terms close to untrammelled or unmediated 'neoliberalism'. Associated with advocacy organisations such as the Club for Growth and think-tanks such as the Heritage Foundation and the Cato Institute it largely rests upon supply-side economics. Economic conservatism is thus associated with calls for marginal and average tax reductions, deregulation, the promotion of entrepreneurship, trade liberalisation and the cutting back of government so that, as one prominent apparatchik put it, it could be drowned in the bathtub. Although, as noted above, the Reagan administration only embraced policies such as these episodically, economic conservatives represent themselves as the most legitimate heirs to the Reagan legacy.

Cultural or religious conservatism, which has over the decades been represented through organisations and networks such as the Moral Majority, the Christian Coalition and the Family Research Council, has a different starting point. It represents the US as a Judeo-Christian nation in terms of its historic roots and stresses the defining role of moral issues such as abortion, traditional marriage, embryonic stem-cell research, pornography and 'abstinence-only' sex education. By implication at least, moral principle and the integrity of the social order take precedence over market forces.

For its part, neo-conservatism or 'national security conservatism' pointed to the political and philosophical principles upon which the US was constructed and encapsulated in founding documents such as the Declaration of Independence. It promoted the case for an assertive foreign policy based upon the spreading of these principles that it saw as encapsulated in democracy and the free market. The argument was partly moral and partly strategic. The founding principles of the US provided liberty to which all were entitled. Furthermore, it was said, democracies generally did not resolve their differences through war or spread terrorism. It thus offered the vista of a more peaceful world. To some degree at least, neo-conservatism informed the Bush administration's 2003 decision to invade Iraq and topple Saddam Hussein. The creation of a stable, democratic Iraq would, it was said, lay a basis for the transformation of the entire region and its democratisation. In sum, 'neocons' claimed at the time, 'the road to Jerusalem lies through Baghdad' (Kemp, 2004).

While there were tensions between these strands, there were also, however, substantial ideational overlaps. Indeed, few individuals or groupings were in practice unequivocally identified with a single conservative current. Although there were libertarians within the ranks of economic conservatives who saw more or less no legitimate role for government in the regulation of moral order, most economic conservatives regarded traditional morality as a necessary underpinning for the proper functioning of markets. Similarly, cultural conservatives saw 'big government' as a threat to the family and community and therefore backed efforts to secure tax and spending reductions. It is fair to conclude that contemporary Republicanism was built around an implicit pact or understanding through which each of these currents agreed to back or at least tolerate the other currents' core concerns. Certainly, John Judis has made the claim:

> There was an implicit arrangement by which the major business lobbies would acquiesce in Republican opposition to abortion, gun control, or affirmative action in exchange for working-class support for reductions in regulations and taxes. (Judis, 2016: 43)

Embeddedness

Nonetheless, although the Republicans were relatively united as a party, securing presidential, Congressional and state-level victories, and often appeared to be *hegemonic*, all three strands of thinking were more shallowly embedded than it often appeared. Some policy ideas (such as cutting welfare or imposing tough law and order policies) generally secured widespread support and there are, as noted in Chapter 2, long-standing suspicions of government. However, backing for some other conservative policies was limited and conditional. Public support for large-scale tax cuts was always accompanied by a degree of bitterness towards the highest-earning elites and what were seen as excessive inequalities. Often, distinctions were drawn between legitimate and illegitimate forms of wealth. Polls suggest for example that the wealth acquired by the banking sector and the multinational corporations was regarded as illegitimate particularly when set against that accumulated by small or family businesses. Furthermore, cultural issues such as abortion or sexual activity outside the bonds of marriage were always regarded more equivocally by much of the public than the 'religious right' would have wished and over the decades there was growing support for gay and lesbian rights. Neo-conservatism and its efforts to 'export' democracy had even shallower roots. Although there had been majority support for the US-led invasion of Iraq while it appeared to offer the prospect of a swift victory, opinion quickly turned to opposition. By the end of 2005, as Iraq became a military and political quagmire, Gallup polling suggested that 59 per cent of Americans regarded the venture as a mistake (Dugan, 2013).

The white working class

There was another process that should be set alongside and considered together with the shallowly embedded character of conservatism. They both contribute to an understanding of the reasons why the Trump insurgency was to prove victorious in 2016.

The Republican Party secured many of its electoral successes because there was a long-running process of partisan realignment. The 'New Deal coalition' of voters, built in the 1930s around Franklin Roosevelt's successive electoral successes, drew in the white working class alongside its other constituent groupings.

Over time, however, there were defections amongst whites and by 1980, when Ronald Reagan was first elected, 61 per cent of whites without a college education voted for him. The numbers were lower amongst higher-income whites (thereby reordering traditional textbook cleavages through which those on lower incomes support the more left-wing party) but he gained 52 per cent support across the white population as a whole. Four years later, the figures were even higher when Reagan secured a landslide re-election victory. The numbers fell back in the 1990s during the Clinton era because the Republican presidential vote was split by Ross Perot's candidatures, the New Democrats had tacked rightwards, and the economic upswing had boosted real incomes. Nonetheless, white working-class support for the Republicans rose again when George W. Bush, John McCain and Mitt Romney respectively headed the ticket. Indeed, 57 per cent of all white voters backed Romney in 2012.

Given these numbers, the white working class can be regarded as a core Republican constituency. Certainly in recent decades the party's electoral successes have depended upon its votes. Why did this happen? There are different reasons. Many southern whites abandoned the Democrats because of the party's associations with civil rights legislation in the 1960s and, over time, the shift away from the Democrats to the Republicans trickled down from presidential candidates to Congressional and state races. Republican presidential candidates also secured crossover votes by stressing national security issues and decrying what they framed as the Democrats' associations with leftist constituencies (the Democratic Party was tarred with the claim that it stood for 'acid, amnesty and abortion' in 1972). The 'culture war' may also have been a factor. In his book, *What's the matter with Kansas?*, Thomas Frank pointed to the role that cultural issues such as same-sex marriage and dislike of 'liberal elites' played in pushing white working-class voters away from the Democrats and towards the Republicans. There was, however, a paradox. By backing the Republicans, Frank argued, such voters were allowing the imposition of policies based upon the free market and fiscal conservatism that might have served the interests of those with substantial income and wealth but were profoundly damaging for those very voters, many of whom were on lower rungs of the economic ladder (Frank, 2005).

Nonetheless, although the white working class, particularly those who came to be dubbed 'angry white men', became an important and visible part of the Republicans' electoral bloc, they have, despite their numerical weight, always been under-represented when it came to the party's nominees particularly at presidential level. In recent Republican primaries the sections of the white working class that participated in the Republican nominating process have, in the absence of credible alternatives, thrown their electoral weight behind 'outsider' candidates such as former Pennsylvania Senator Rick Santorum or Governor Mike Huckabee who then went on to defeat at the hands of 'establishment' party figures such as Senator John McCain or Governor Mitt Romney. Although primarily associated with religious conservatism and moral issues, both Santorum and Huckabee sought to navigate the divide between the white working-class electorate and the 'culture wars' politics of the Christian right. They spoke in quasi-populist terms and pointed to the impact of economic forces on traditional working-class communities while at the same time highlighting and campaigning around moral issues.

Populist discourses

The increasing weight of the white working class within the Republican Party's constituencies, the shallowly embedded character of the three strands that defined US conservatism, and the visible but contained place of economically populist discourses within Republicanism, opened the way and set the stage for Donald Trump's 2016 election campaign.

Although he at times presented himself as a transactional businessman and deal-maker and at other points embraced contemporary Republican orthodoxies, Trump's campaign was very largely structured, as noted in Chapter 3, around right-wing populism. Having said that, populism is of course a term that is more frequently used than defined. There are also difficulties associated with its use. This is because here are very significant differences in the forms that populism takes in different national and historical settings. South American populism has a long history that is strikingly different to the expressions of populism in North America and Europe. And there have been important, left-leaning populist movements in the US, most notably at the end of the nineteenth century when small farmers organised against the big city elites, banking interests, the railroad corporations and the gold standard. Arguably, the Occupy Wall Street movement that emerged in 2011 inherited or resurrected this tradition.

These wide differences between different forms of populism exist because it is much more a guiding sentiment or a political logic rather than a distinct or set ideology (Judis, 2016: 14). Often it provides an edge for ideologies. Even when it overshadows the more structured ideologies nested within it, populism has a 'thin' rather than a 'thick' conceptual core (Kriesi and Pappas, 2016: 4). It is, by definition, blurred and indistinct.

Nonetheless, having said that, some conclusions can be drawn about the character of contemporary populism in both the US and Europe. By definition, populism rests upon claims to identify with the 'people' who, in its representations, not only possess moral purity encompassing for example honesty, integrity and a commitment to genuine work and enterprise but are invariably pitched against exploitative, manipulative and self-serving elites. At times, this suspicion of elite manipulation and corruption is such that populist critiques spill over into conspiracy theories.

By implication the populist commitment to the 'people' is anti-pluralist in character. Because the people are seen as one it follows that they can thus have only one truly legitimate representative or party speaking and acting on their behalf (Müller, 2016: 20). Nonetheless, that having been said, only *some* people form part of the people. This is because, first, the elites are by definition separate and distinct from the people. Second, there are undeserving and marginalised groupings that also lie outside the people's ranks. Such groupings are defined by, for example, the character of their employment, their place of origin, race, ethnicity, gender, sexuality, politics or perhaps educational qualifications (populism has generally incorporated a marked anti-intellectualism and a pronounced hostility to the media industry). Thus, military veterans are part of the people (because of their service to the nation) while others who might also be reduced to begging do not form part of the people. In these accounts, while some newcomers may be 'invisible' because they share racial origins and language with the host society, most immigrant groupings are also external to the people and of course they constitute a primary target of populist hostility. Indeed, against a background of economic malaise, immigration has of course become a principal driver, perhaps *the* primary driver, of contemporary right-wing populism in both Europe and the US.

There is a further twist. Right-wing populist representations often suggest that the elites and marginal groups are bound together by common intent or purposes: they 'discern a symbiotic relationship between an elite that does not truly belong and marginal groups that are also distinct from the people' (Müller, 2016: 23). Accounts often suggest, for example, that immigration is encouraged because 'globalist' political and commercial elites are seeking to undermine or 'dilute' the nation-state and the people.

All this is in turn overlain by anxieties and concerns about openness in all its forms as well as the uncertainty and fluidity that accompanies openness. Although some campaigning for the 2016 Brexit vote held out the promise of the UK as an independent and open state, many others in their ranks had a far more insular vision. In particular, they resented the migration patterns that EU membership entailed.

Populist resistance to openness is generally tied to its visions of the nation. Indeed, contemporary right-wing populism sees the 'people' and the nation as indissoluble. The nation is a 'natural' component of human affairs. Thus the populist project seeks the salvation and resurrection of the nation-state as a basis for human order and the nation has to be rescued from the clutches of globalist elites. Indeed, populist discourses suggest a relentless search for the 'imagined community' that forms the basis of nations (Anderson, 2016). Ann Coulter, the well-known conservative commentator who vigorously backed the Trump campaign, reduced the 2016 presidential election to a battle between globalism and nationality (Hains, 2016). It was an over-simplification but it contained more than a grain of truth.

Having said that, contemporary right-wing populism celebrates the nation-state, its representations of the nation are pulled between ethnic or racial and civic definitions of the nation. At one end of the continuum, populist claims fuse with white nationalism. They assert that there is an American nation-state based upon white northern and western European folkways. At the other end of the continuum, populist accounts provide a more open vision of the nation but it is still one that imposes 'loyalty tests' and makes demands upon those who seek admission. Seen from this perspective, newcomers must not only integrate but also assimilate.

All these political claims are tied to certain understandings of economic processes. Populist accounts have often tied their defence of the nation-state to critiques of what they depict as exploitative or unfair economic arrangements imposed by multinational and supranational elite forces. At times, in the past, they have cited the gold standard and many contemporary populist accounts are structured around a condemnation of trade liberalisation and globalising processes. These, it is said, have allowed unfairly privileged elites to benefit illegitimately from the labours of the people (Brewer, 2016: 251). At the same time, there is a *producerist* strand in populist thinking. This draws a distinction between productive and unproductive capital. The former refers to capital that serves the people, particularly small firms, while the latter incorporates the financial sector, in particular the 'hedge fund guys' as Trump called them, and the 'stateless' multinational corporations. Thus, in the closing weeks of the 2016 campaign, Trump was able to exploit the revelations about the content of Hillary Clinton's speeches to companies such as Goldman Sachs, Deutsche Bank and GE very effectively so as to highlight her elite connections.

Defining themes

As has been noted, populism has a long history in the US. In building upon and reproducing earlier right-wing populist frames, the Trump campaign structured itself, in particular, around eight defining but interlinking and overlapping themes.

First, while conspiracy theories are, as has been seen, never far from the surface in populist thinking they were particularly pronounced in Trump's claims and statements. Early in the primary season Trump posed questions about the death of Supreme Court Justice Antonin Scalia and appeared to suggest that Senator Ted Cruz's father had been implicated in the Kennedy assassination (Brewer, 2016: 259). More significantly, Trump had, prior to the beginnings of this campaign and while it was under way, used Birtherism, a prototypical conspiracy theory, to deny the legitimacy of the Obama presidency and thereby at the same time tarnish Hillary Clinton as a candidate. Indeed, it provided him with the starting point for his campaign.[2]

'Birtherism' was structured around the claim that Obama had been born outside the US, probably in Kenya and was therefore ineligible for the presidency; this was in turn closely allied to the proposition that he was a 'secret Muslim'. By 2011, Trump had established himself as the country's most prominent representative of the Birther creed and although his statements were often framed as questions of assertions of uncertainty they appeared to rest on these racially tinged representations of Obama as an outsider who lacked connections with or roots in the US. Trump asserted:

> Our current president came out of nowhere. Came out of nowhere ... In fact, I'll go a step further: The people that went to school with him, they never saw him, they don't know who he is. It's crazy. (Quoted in Prokop, 2016a)

While Birtherism never won a majority following, its claims nonetheless spread widely and secured a significant audience particularly within the core of the Tea Party movement. In April 2010, a *New York Times* / CBS News survey asked respondents to state their beliefs about Obama's place of birth. The findings suggested that amongst the general population 20 per cent believed that he had been born outside of the US. Amongst self-declared Tea Party supporters, the figure was almost a third (30 per cent) (*New York Times* / CBS News, 2010: 24). This is of course a minority but the evidence suggests that those who were most committed to the movement were those most firmly attached to Birtherism. Another survey conducted two years later in 2012 showed that 55.8 per cent of those who described themselves as 'strong' Tea Party supporters believed that the president had been born abroad (Aberbach, 2017: 92).[3] For these activists, President Obama was, in effect, an unconstitutional and illegitimate interloper.

Other conspiracy theories emerged from within the Trump campaign as Election Day approached. The election system was, he repeatedly asserted, rigged. At times it was said to be rigged because Hillary Clinton had been permitted to contest the election when she should have been imprisoned. At other points, and there was perhaps some reality to this claim, it was rigged because much of the media opposed his candidacy. And then again Trump suggested that the voting system would be manipulated.

Furthermore, the suspicion of 'globalism' that defines contemporary populism was ever present. These references to globalism appear akin to the concept of a 'new world order', orchestrated by elite interests and supranational institutions so as to strip away freedoms and destroy nations, which has long been a centrepiece of far right discourses. As in many accounts, globalist designs are tied to finance capital.[4] A Trump campaign advertisement pointed to banking cabals. Arguably such claims, like the well-worn phrase 'new world order', have an anti-Semitic edge:

> Hillary Clinton meets in secret with international banks to plot the destruction of U.S. sovereignty in order to enrich these global financial powers, her special interest friends and her donors. (Chokshi, 2016)

Second, Trump's candidacy was defined by immigration. In campaign statements, legal immigration was often blurred together with both illegal immigration and representations of particular countries or regions of the world. As Trump announced his candidacy, he anchored it in comments about Mexicans and the call for the building of a border wall. In words that have been widely reproduced he said: 'When Mexico sends its people, they're not sending their best .... They're bringing drugs. They're bringing crime. They're rapists. And some, I assume, are good people' (*Washington Post*, 2015). He then went on to make his calls for the construction of a 'beautiful' and 'impenetrable' border wall, which, it was repeatedly said, Mexico would fund, and the creation of a 'deportation task force' within Immigration and Customs Enforcement (ICE). This was an important rallying cry in itself but the border wall also had symbolic value insofar as it represented the reclaiming of American sovereignty.

The process of ideational 'entrepreneurship' – and Trump can surely be regarded as an ideational entrepreneur – goes beyond simple statements of policy, their creative packaging, and the use of simple, exaggerated claims so as to secure attention. It requires the creation of narratives and the pitching of cognitive and normative ideas in ways that will win a substantial share of the ideational market. Whereas the selling of policy ideas at elite level often requires what might be regarded as precision crafting and 'nano-targeting' towards particular epistemic communities, the selling of ideas to a broader audience 'is often less related to their analytic skills than to the broad mass intuitions of the moment' (Widmaier, Blyth and Seabrooke, 2007: 755).

Such intuitions can come about, as Leonard Seabrooke suggests when there is a 'legitimacy gap' (or an increasing 'legitimacy gap') between elite perceptions and preferences and 'the broader population's intersubjective understandings' (Seabrooke, 2005: 3). For example, the opening up of such a legitimacy gap around economic policy in the UK during the inter-war years paved the way for economic policy experiments that began to depart from laissez-faire orthodoxies. During the 1920s there were increased expectations around housing, leisure and living standards that were frustrated by economic circumstances (Seabrooke, 2007: 797). Similarly, the raising of consumer aspirations and expectations during the long period preceding the 2008–2009 economic crisis and stagnating real incomes (and the fall in the years following the crisis) created a legitimacy gap that the Trump campaign very successfully tapped.

Effective ideational entrepreneurship requires more than creativity and opportunity.[5] It also demands the 'creative destruction' (to use Joseph Schumpeter's term) of older or competing sets of ideas (Watts, Holbrook and Smith, 2015: 19). Schumpeter was referring to changes in economic structures as new forms of production incessantly displaced the old but the concept can also be applied to ideational 'production' (Schumpeter, 1994: 82). Thus, ideational entrepreneurship fuses the generation and framing of ideas with the destruction, or at least marginalisation, of the old.

The destruction and marginalisation of the old fused together with Trump's more or less continuous use of hyperbole. Together with a style that he pioneered on *The Apprentice* and a persona that fitted the structures of reality television, it all won Trump very substantial free media coverage.[6] Indeed, some saw Trump's rise as confirmation of the Frankfurt School's claim that the culture industry, from which he emerged, played the determining role in shaping the public imagination. Certainly, Trump's media role and his celebrity status provided him with an entry point into the social media enabling him to acquire over 17 million Twitter followers. Twitter proved to be a medium that played an important part in allowing Trump to set the agenda and in some ways also lent itself to the authoritarian style of politics that Trump pursued. The limit of 140 characters facilitates and promotes the abrupt assertion in place of dialogue or more considered forms of political discourse.

Social media were so important to the campaign because they displaced the long-established gatekeepers associated with the 'mainstream media' thereby giving Trump freer rein. This facilitated his 'anti-politics' style, the bringing forth of new policies, and the making of statements way outside of the bounds of conventional political or inter-personal norms. This, in turn, created uncertainty within the established or 'mainstream' media about the ways in which they should cover Trump's assertions and claim leading to assertions that they played a role in normalising and legitimising his candidacy and the politics around which it was structured. Thus, in sum, the rise of new social media may have enabled the Trump campaign to move what has been dubbed the 'Overton window', the framework of policy options regarded as acceptable or legitimate at any given moment, fairly easily:

> Mr. Trump's rise is actually a symptom of the mass media's growing weakness, especially in controlling the limits of what it is acceptable to say ... For worse, and sometimes for better, the Overton window is broken. We are in an era of rapidly weakening gatekeepers. (Tufekci, 2016)

Third, Trump's populism focused on Islam and the consequences, as he portrayed them, of Muslim immigration. In December 2015, following shootings in San Bernardino, California, Trump brought Muslim immigration to the fore:

> Donald J. Trump is calling for a total and complete shutdown of Muslims entering the United States until our country's representatives can figure out what is going on. (*Associated Press*, 2016)

At times, the character of his discourses edged towards the frames adopted in parts of northern Europe by right-wing populist parties whereby anti-Islamic politics are represented largely in terms of what is portrayed as Islamic opposition to western progressiveness and cultural liberalism. Six months after San Bernardino, in June 2016, Trump drew upon the shootings in an Orlando club so as to offer himself, as some European populist parties had done, as a guarantor of western progressivism. In doing so, he very forcefully broke ranks with religious conservatives within the Republican orbit who continued to campaign against efforts to normalise gay and lesbian relationships. For Trump: 'a radical Islamic terrorist targeted the nightclub, not only because he wanted to kill Americans, but in order to execute gay and lesbian citizens, because of their sexual orientation' (quoted in Beckwith, 2016).

Fourth, Trump's populism drew, to some degree at least, on what is known in the US as 'operational liberalism'. In Europe, it is social democracy. Despite a broad commitment to limited, 'constitutional' government, many grassroots conservatives and certainly those in the ranks of Trump's 2016 electorate were either opposed to, or certainly did not support, cuts to government 'entitlement' programmes such as Social Security and Medicare (while being much less favourable to 'welfare' benefits and Medicaid). This is a long-time strain within the American right. Interviews with supporters of the Tea Party movement, many of whom went on to form the battalions behind the Trump campaign, reveal that although there was hostility to 'big government' as an abstract or generalised proposition, and support for increases in spending fell markedly between 2008 and 2012, there was relatively little appetite for cuts in many areas of spending (Aberbach, 2017: 52).

Nonetheless, there is a divide on this between grassroots sentiments and economic conservatives. For those who placed their faith in market forces, entitlement spending had to be scaled back and reconfigured. It was no longer economically viable. For example, House Speaker Paul Ryan had put forward plans for the partial privatisation of Medicare.

Yet, in striking contrast to Republican elites, the Trump campaign echoed grassroots sentiments and in a promise that may have played a part in winning white working-class votes said in tones that were sometimes equivocal and sometimes definite, it would protect these programmes. This gave the campaign, at least at times, a leftist hue in the same way as the European populist parties sometimes appear to talk in terms more usually associated with social democracy. Although in part a tongue-in-cheek exercise, an op-ed column in *The Washington Post* suggested that when taken together, Trump's policies towards state social provision and migration resembled those being pursued in Denmark, a country that had been hailed as a model that the US should emulate by Senator Bernie Sanders in his prolonged bid to wrest the Democratic Party presidential nomination from Hillary Clinton:

> the package Trump offers – 'save Social Security without cuts,' a vaguely pro-single-payer position on health care, plus temporarily banning Muslims and walling off Mexico – bears an eerie resemblance to the Danish government's current policy mix. (Lane, 2016)

Fifth, whereas Republicanism had since about 1970 been associated with trade liberalisation and had backed free trade agreements much more resolutely than the Democrats who had often been pulled in different directions, Trump structured his campaign around vehement opposition to offshoring, threatening a 35 per cent tariff on companies moving their operations abroad and denunciations of prevailing trade arrangements and impending trade agreements. He targeted the 1992–1993 North American Free Trade Agreement (NAFTA) (which he wanted amended) and the Trans-Pacific Partnership (TPP) (which he wanted abandoned) that had at the time of the 2016 campaign been negotiated but not agreed by Congress (Ashbee and Waddan 2010). Trump repeatedly pointed to the transfer of jobs from the US to Mexico and what he saw as Chinese currency manipulation so as to reduce the prices of their exports. Chinese products would, he promised, be subject to tariffs of up to 45 per cent. Manufacturing, he promised, would be restored to the American heartlands.[7]

Sixth, Trump's vision rested at times on what can be regarded as 'crony capitalism' or, put less pejoratively, market relationships heavily mediated by personal connections and favour-based networks. It is this, as well as his populist appeals, that triggered the comparisons with the former Italian Prime Minister, Silvio Berlusconi. 'Crony capitalism' is of course both a contested and pejorative term. The libertarian right would for example deny that capitalism can ever take a 'crony' form insofar as they would assert that it is by definition based upon freely operating markets rather than private networks. Nonetheless, Trump's vision of capitalism seems to be strongly tainted by cronyism insofar as there are frequent hints of clientelism and the granting of selective favours to particular firms, while at the same time the dividing line between Trump's politics and his business empire often appeared blurred and indistinct. These perceptions were strengthened in December 2016 when, as President-Elect, Trump announced the conclusion of an agreement based upon incentives and perhaps some threats with Carrier Air Conditioner, a division of United Technologies that kept some jobs in Indiana that would otherwise have been transferred to Mexico. For libertarian commentators, deals with individual firms did not bode well. As Tyler Cowen said: 'This to me is scary ... It indicates an environment where business decisions are now about how much you please the president' (National Public Radio, 2016).

Trump eschewed both the neo-conservative foreign policy vision of an American mission to reshape the globe and the governing principles of the post-1945 order that the Republicans as well as Democrats had with only a few exceptions championed. Instead, he resurrected the slogan of 'America First' (a conscious or unconscious appropriation of the isolationist, and perhaps pro-German, effort to keep the US from joining the Second World War) and called for a crude big-power Realism. Although at times Trump simply seemed to be calling on US allies to contribute more to their own defence, he at other times appeared to redefine US strategic interests away from the post-1945 consensus so that they were much narrower in scope. Threats such as ISIS would be quickly dispatched and the armed forces would be increased in size but there would at the same time be a retreat from the principle of collective security and treaty obligations such as those imposed by NATO. Smaller states, it seemed at times, could no longer shelter under the American umbrella. Although he professed a commitment to Israel (and the relocation of the US Embassy to Jerusalem), he seemed much more equivocal at other points. And there always appeared to be respect, seemingly based upon a shared commitment to nationalism and abrasive Realism, for both Vladimir Putin's Russia and Putin himself.

Seventh, all of this was tied to a fierce populist resentment of, and hostility to, many (although far from all) established elites and, in particular, the 'political class'. The defining purpose of his election campaign, Trump said, was to 'drain the Washington swamp' (*Los Angeles Times*, 2016). The 'swamp' seemed to encompass legislators, government employees and lobbyists working on behalf of 'special interests'. The hostility to the 'political class' was not only reflected in the assaults upon 'political correctness' which was then used as leverage with which to raise issues relating to race, ethnicity and gender but also in the strident hostility towards Hillary Clinton that often went well beyond the known bounds of conventional political discourse. Whereas Trump framed himself in terms of 'anti-politics', Clinton was the consummate political insider. She represented continuity with not only the Obama years but also her husband's administrations during the 1990s. The cries of 'lock her up' became an integral and institutionalised feature of Trump's campaign rallies. Trump himself said:

> The criminal conduct of Hillary Clinton threatens the foundations of democracy ... This is our last chance ... This is bigger than me or any of us. It's about our country. This is about restoring our Constitution. (Quoted in Berenson and Frizell, 2016)

Eighth, all of this was bound together with the promise of restoration. The slogan 'Make America Great Again', seemingly appropriated from the 1980 Reagan campaign, offered a return to a past age. In part this was about framing. Representations of unspecified past 'greatness' seemed to evoke images of a *pax Americana*, ordered stability and a patriotic nation seemingly untroubled by dissent and division. However, 'Make America Great Again' also had a 'material' basis. From about 1970 onwards, the white working class had taken an economic and social battering. This not only involved the loss of job opportunities. The labour force participation rate appears to have declined for other reasons. In a typical north-eastern white working-class community about 9 per cent of 20 to 64 year-old males were outside the workforce in 1960. By 2000, the figure had risen to 30 per cent (Murray, 2013: 220). Community cohesion and social capital declined. And while the seeming stability of mid-twentieth-century marriages may have hidden many secrets and miseries, relationships and parenting seemed under threat as the century came to a close

(Murray, 2013). Significantly, data suggest that Trump scored his biggest general election successes compared with Mitt Romney's candidacy four years previously in counties with the highest drug, alcohol and suicide mortality rates (Hohmann, 2016). In sum, the Trump campaign tapped a vein when it spoke, as it did repeatedly, of restoring what white America had lost.

Strongman and *caudillismo* politics

All these themes and policy issues may, however, be secondary. Arguably, something else was at work. Throughout his campaign, Trump painted a particularly dark vision of the US and the world. It appeared that the country was under siege by enemies foreign and domestic. It hung on the edge of survival.

Against this background, Trump not only spoke of policy change but perhaps more importantly put himself forward as a strongman. He was not a conventional candidate but at the helm of a movement (although it was of course highly unstructured). Challenges would be addressed and swiftly resolved through his own judgements and actions. Unlike conventional politicians he would not be beholden to others. Furthermore, through the nature of his claims and his rhetoric that proved to be the antithesis of Obama's sometimes laborious and often nuanced 'professorial' style, he offered an assurance of certainty.

There were other hallmarks of the strongman approach. Trump's rallies were often marked, as Hillary Clinton's campaign ads highlighted, by implicit and explicit threats of violence. There was a particular animus towards the media and their representatives. And he seemed at times to question the legitimacy of dissent, the incumbent president and other election candidates.

Some survey data reveals that Trump drew particularly strong support from authoritarian voters who are looking for just such a leader. Such voters attach particular importance to, for example, bringing up children to be respectful and obedient. At the beginning of the election year 43 per cent of strong authoritarians who defined themselves as Republicans backed

Trump. Authoritarianism may also contribute to an explanation of his general election victory. The same poll found that 39 per cent of independents were authoritarians and 17 per cent of Democrats could be categorised as 'strong authoritarians' (MacWilliams, 2016). Such authoritarianism may in part be a response to the long-running decline of trust. Whereas, in May 1972, some 75 per cent of Americans had expressed 'a great deal' or a 'fair amount' of trust in government the figure was 49 per cent in September 2016 (Gallup, 2016).

Others have also noted the 'strongman' component within Trump's political persona. An op-ed column in *The Financial Times* drew a comparison between Trump and figures such as Egypt's Abdel Fattah al-Sisi and Turkey's Recep Tayyip Erdogan:

> All these men have promised to lead a national revival through the force of their personalities and their willingness to ignore liberal niceties. In many cases, the promise of decisive leadership is backed up by a willingness – sometimes explicit, sometimes implied – to use illegal violence against enemies of the state (Rachman, 2016)

The parallels with South American *caudillismo* are even more strikingly evident. Such parallels are both political and personal. Juan Perón used nationalism to build a base amongst the *descamisados* (shirtless ones) in Argentina. The South American leaders cultivated clientelistic networks and drew their families, as well as younger wives and mistresses (who also played a role in bolstering an aura of power), into the governing process (Vacano, 2016).

It has been argued that populism does not sit easily with authoritarianism (Brewer, 2016: 260). In their efforts to facilitate expressions of the people's will, European populist parties have often supported the extensive use of referendums rather than more deliberative forms of democracy. And American populism has sometimes emphasised its antagonism to federal forms of government and echoed calls for 'states' rights' (Brewer, 2016: 252). Nonetheless, it is also the case that over the years US populism (and certainly Latin American populism) has coexisted relatively easily with authoritarian figures. Huey Long, the Louisiana Governor and Senator who had presidential ambitions, centralised state authority in his own hands. Alabama Governor George Wallace's campaigns were not only laced with diehard support for the manifest authoritarianism of segregation but also rested on calls for vigorous law and order policies. Wallace's comments on the protests and demonstrations that took place in 1968 are illustrative of his style: 'If any demonstrator ever lies down in front of my car, it'll be the last car he'll ever lay down in front of' (quoted in Lind, 2016). It should be added that populism always brings forth an inherent impatience with routine democratic procedures and systems based upon checks and balances. From a populist perspective, the people have the right to cut through these constraints and, because the people have one voice, quickly dispatch dissent that is by definition illegitimate or at most only partially legitimate. There is thus an inherent illiberalism and authoritarianism based on a desire for order and the imposition of leadership. The degree to which they become manifest depends upon the character of the particular settings within which populism comes to the fore (Kriesi and Pappas, 2016: 5; Heinö, 2016: 10). They certainly ran through many of Trump's campaign pronouncements.

There is thus another reason, beyond the reliance on cues noted above, why the specific content of Trump's campaign statements was of less significance than it might be supposed. Arguably, in a strongman movement or regime, supporters are not looking for a campaign platform on which an elected politician will at a later date be judged. Neither are they searching for detailed technocratic plans of the type with which Hillary Clinton became synonymous. They were instead seeking a personality who would respond to events and developments in a decisive and resolute way. Thus while the media took Trump 'literally, but not seriously; his supporters take him seriously, but not literally' (Zito, 2016).

There is a further aspect to Trump's particular form of strongman populism. Some strongmen have styled their image around a personal denial of material rewards. They have stressed their dedication to the people through self-sacrifice. Yet, although Trump stated that he would not take the presidential salary, he nonetheless built his image and personality around his wealth and the most conspicuous forms of consumption.

There is of course a paradox here. As more than a few have said, Trump was hardly in the ranks of the 'ordinary' Americans that he, and the populist discourses he promoted, invoked as the basis for his campaign. Yet, as Jan-Werner Müller notes, despite its opposition to established elites populism in both Europe and the US accepts other elites. It coexists and in some ways embraces elites if they seem to be distanced from the existing (and corrupted) structures of power and appear to promise fealty to the 'people':

> what matters is their promise that as a proper elite, they will not betray the people's trust and will in fact faithfully execute the people's unambiguously articulated political agenda. (Müller, 2016: 30)

At times, and there may well be tensions or indeed clashes between the ideas that cluster together so as to define campaigns and movements, populism celebrates the wealth or connections that its leaders possess. Certainly, interviews with supporters suggest a fascination with Trump's properties and acquisitions and an admiration for his lifestyle.

Much the same could of course be said about Silvio Berlusconi, whose policies sometimes had a distinctly populist edge to them, although Trump may have also gained an advantage from US attitudes towards wealth. Despite the long economic malaise and concern about inequality Roper Center research suggests that most Americans still have faith in a version of the 'American dream'. There remains, it is said, potential for economic mobility. Almost 80 per cent of survey respondents told the pollsters that individuals acquire wealth through different forms of personal effort. Fewer than one in ten believed that it came down to personal connections, family background, natural ability or chance (Roper Center for Public Opinion Research, 2015).

The Alt-Right and paleo-conservatism

Populism and strongman politics only, however, provide a partial description of the thinking associated with Trump and his 2016 campaign. It should be remembered that populism is a set of sentiments rather than a distinct ideology and therefore does not exist in a 'pure' form. Instead, it colours ideologies or alternatively ideologies are nested within within broader, less defined clusters of populist sentiments.

Alongside populism, Trump's thinking appears at times to owe a debt to ideas traditionally associated with paleo-conservatism, the 'Alt-Right', and to some degree the white nationalist right. Certainly they claimed a strong affinity with Trump and sought to bolster, in particular, the commitments that he made to deport illegal immigrants and build a wall on the Mexican border.

'Paleos' (many of whom are associated with the Rockford Institute, *Chronicles* magazine and *The American Conservative*) are informed by a sense of an American identity based not upon a belief in, or attachment to, principle (as neoconservatives insist) but instead upon European tradition and culture.[8] Such tradition was not a high culture but instead structured around attitudes, mores and habits.

Paleo-conservative thinking is informed by a strong sense of lost community based around what might be termed an 'imagined township'. Paleos seek a renegotiation and restructuring of the collective identity upon which the contemporary US rests and the restoration of a past age. From this perspective, there is an American ethnicity (and the US is therefore a *nation*-state) based upon white European folkways.

Paleos would also acknowledge a debt to the former Confederate states and the secessionist cause. While many observers see the Confederacy as built upon racial supremacy paleos understand the antebellum American south as a challenge to the relentless advance of industrial capitalism. Seen in this way, unrestrained market forces fragmented and destabilised the social order in the north. Capitalism placed the worship of profit and money above all else including the integrity of peoples of nations. In contrast, the south had been 'the last nonmaterial civilization in the western world' (quoted in Ashbee, 2000: 78). Thus, the reclaiming and reassertion of American national identity is perceived, to some degree at least, as anti-capitalist. There is certainly, paleo-conservatism would assert, a tension between efforts to preserve or rebuild a white ethnicity and identity and the market.

Given all of this, the Declaration of Independence (1776) and the US Constitution (1787) have much less of a role than that accorded to them by almost all other American political traditions. For paleo-conservatism, the US was not constructed around ideas and principles. Thus, the Declaration and the Constitution should only be considered as 'artifacts of the American experience: they were made by Americans: they did not make America' (quoted in Ashbee, 2000: 76).

The paleo-conservative commitment to a US informed by, and structured around, European folkways as well as notions of community and an embrace of the 'lost cause' lead to an emphasis upon immigration and protectionism. Paleos cite the destruction of the Rust Belt towns and cities as well as the impact of migration and the changing demographic face of the US as the white (non-Hispanic) population has diminished and continues to diminish as a proportion of the overall population. There is thus an ideational overlap between paleo-conservatism, the white nationalist right and race-based and more overtly agitational websites such VDARE (named after a child, said to be the first born to English settler parents on the American continent).

VDARE pioneered the argument behind the electoral strategy that the Trump campaign came to embrace. Writing at the end of 2000, Steve Sailer, a VDARE contributor, pointed out that George W. Bush had, in that year's presidential election, gained only 54 per cent of the white vote. Even a relatively small increase would, Sailer argued, ensure Republican victories. Such an increase could be secured by bringing the issue of immigration to the forefront, thereby splitting many white workers from the unions and the Democrats (Sailer, 2000).

All of this creates a sharp dividing line between paleo-conservatism and its allies on one hand and on the other hand the dominant strands within American conservatism over the past half-century. In paleo eyes, economic conservatism is regarded as an ideological tool that, through its promotion of trans-nationalism, serves the interests of a multinational class and managerial elites that are detached from the American nation and its interests. While paleo-conservatism is committed to the market, and there is a paleo-libertarian sub-strand based around the Ludwig von Mises Institute in Auburn, Alabama that has at times edged towards anarcho-capitalism, it sees an important role for the state in structuring the social order and setting a framework for market activity.

Having said this, 'paleos' have a much closer attachment to state rather than federal government. There is an overlap with neo-confederate thinking here and a corresponding stress upon the importance of 'states rights'. It has thus been said that whereas some conservatives look back to an era before Lyndon Johnson's presidency, which enlarged government very considerably, and others seek the restoration of the US as it was in the years before Franklin Roosevelt and the New Deal, 'paleos' seek an American nation either as it was constituted before the Civil War (1861–1865) or indeed before the US Constitution was written (1787) and the thirteen original states were governed by the Articles of Confederation of 1781.

Paleo-conservatism is also divided from the ranks of the 'religious right'. While there are shared sentiments and 'paleos' are certainly on the same side as the religious right in the 'culture wars' that have raged over recent decades, they would distance themselves from the civic conception of US identity that informs Christian cultural conservatism. From a paleo perspective, issues such as abortion and same-sex marriage might be worthy but have proved a distraction from the task of restoring American nationhood and imposing controls upon migration and trade.

There is also a major cleavage if foreign policy and attitudes towards neo-conservatism are considered. Paleo-conservatism understands the US as a republic rather than an empire. In broad terms, its thinking incorporates isolationist sympathies insofar as it would pull back from the US's global commitments and rejects efforts to 'export' democratic principles. In some paleo accounts this goes beyond an abrasive Realism. There is also a particular reluctance to underwrite Israel and a distinct distaste for the East Coast 'Anglo' or White Anglo-Saxon Protestant (WASP) elites that, it has been argued, have drawn the country into European conflicts on Britain's side.[9] It has been said that paleo-conservatism instead has its ideational roots in nineteenth-century migration to the US from countries such as Germany and Ireland. There have thus always been suspicions of the United Kingdom and its imperial associations.

Since its emergence paleo-conservatism has remained at the edges of the conservative movement. Under the editorship of William F. Buckley, *National Review* drew the boundaries of the movement in ways that defined some, including those who were overtly anti-Semitic, the John Birch Society, Patriot and militia groupings, and paleo-conservatism, as being far beyond those boundaries.

Nonetheless, despite Buckley's efforts, Patrick J. Buchanan's presidential bids in the 1990s and his appearances as a television talkshow contributor, went some way towards rehabilitating 'paleo' ideas and certainly made them more visible. Buchanan secured just over 37 per cent of the vote in the 1992 New Hampshire Republican primary thereby unsettling and weakening President George H.W. Bush's re-election effort. Four years later, in 1996, Buchanan went on to win the New Hampshire primary although his campaign then stalled. He later co-founded *The American Conservative*. His books bemoaned the Allies' entry into the Second World War that he deemed an 'unnecessary war' that had opened the way for communist expansionism. At the same time he lambasted immigration and sought to reclaim the protectionist argument for the Republican Party.

As the Trump 2016 campaign developed, the paleo associations became more visible. There was an even more transparent link with the Alt-Right and its constituent parts including the website *Infowars*, the National Policy Institute, the Government

Accountability Institute and the *Alex Jones Show*. The connection between the campaign and the Alt-Right was laid bare when Stephen Bannon was appointed as Trump's campaign chief and then Chief Strategist in the White House. Indeed, the *New York Times* referred in an editorial to 'Donald Trump's Alt-Right Brain' (*New York Times*, 2016). Bannon was formerly executive chairman of *Breitbart News* that is widely seen as a conduit between the Alt-Right and a much wider audience. The Southern Poverty Law Center has suggested that *Breitbart News* turned still further towards the Alt-Right in 2015–2016:

> Over the past year the media outlet has been openly promoting the core issues of the Alt-Right, introducing these racist ideas to its readership – much to the delight of many in the white nationalist world who could never dream of reaching such a vast number of people. (Piggott, 2016)

The relationship between Trump and *Breitbart News* was not simply mediated through Bannon. A study of 26,234 of Trump's tweets and retweets during 2015–2016 showed that he drew upon Breitbart to a much greater extent than 'mainstream' news outlets (Warzel and Vo, 2016).

The 'Alt-Right' (the term is said to have emerged in 2008) might legitimately be regarded as a popularised and crudely popularising form of paleo-conservatism although the political styles are very different.[10] The Alt-Right attracts far younger, largely male, adherents and draws upon vehement hostility to feminism (some adherents talk of a 'manosphere'), the online trolling culture, and a sense of building a counter-culture in ways that appeared to replicate consciously the strategies once pursued by the cultural left.

Having said this, white nationalism and what is sometimes dubbed 'identitarianism' appear to be the single most important starting points for many Alt-Right activists. Indeed, they often embrace nationalism in a far cruder form than 'paleo' outlets. The National Policy Institute, that is generally seen as an important element within the Alt-Right, stated for example that it was 'dedicated to the heritage, identity and future of people of European descent in the United States, and around the world' (*New York Times*, 2016). The Institute held its annual conference in Washington DC just after the 2016 election at which, as press reports noted, featured Nazi salutes (Lombroso and Appelbaum, 2016).

It should be added that Alt-Right publications show little enthusiasm for NATO and, like paleo-conservatives, oppose neoconservative visions of remaking regions of the world. There is evidence of alarm within the Alt-Right when John Bolton, a veteran 'hawk' who served in the Bush administration, was included in lists of potential nominees to be Secretary of State in the Trump administration.

Alt-Right outlets often have a sensationalist and personalising twist resting on the creation and reproduction of internet memes. There is much to be found on its sites that critics would assert is racist, anti-Semitic and misogynistic. Certainly, the Alt-Right seems to relish its role as a *provocateur*. It targets 'political correctness' and the 'establishment' while dismissing its opponents in exuberantly vituperative terms. Other conservatives were dubbed 'cuckolds' from which the terms 'cuckservatives' and 'cucks' were derived in an effort to suggest that they were weak and politically neutered.

Bricolage

As has been emphasised, Trump's thinking represents a sharp break with the ideational currents that have defined conservatism and Republicanism in recent decades. Nonetheless, there were also some continuities. Alongside populism and the themes derived from paleo-conservatism, Trump's campaign also absorbed and reproduced many of the policy ideas as well as the cognitive and normative assumptions underpinning them from more mainstream, post-Reagan forms of Republicanism and conservatism.

The Trump campaign juggled with different clusters of ideas that at times could not be reconciled with each other. Demands for protectionism, measures to stop offshoring, infrastructure spending, controls on migration, a major foreign policy shift as well as strident denunciations of elites and the suggestions of strongman politics thus sat easily with a commitment to free markets, limited government, economic liberty and de-regulation. They overlapped in pledges to reverse the reform measures that had been pursued by the Obama administration through either legislation or unilateral executive action. And, while not elevating moral issues to the position that they had in earlier election contests, Trump endorsed some of the basic principles long associated with religious right constituencies within the Republicans' ranks. Thus, while he had supported pro-choice positions earlier in his life, he announced that he was unambiguously 'pro-life' in 2011 (Aberbach, 2017: 133).[11] However, Trump often seemed unfamiliar with, and uncertain about, the defining planks of religious conservatism. His knowledge of the Bible appeared thin. He sometimes backtracked and at other times went beyond their arguments. In March 2016 Trump appeared to assert that women who had abortions should face criminal penalties (Bump, 2016a). Arguably, the selection of Indiana Governor Mike Pence as the vice-presidential nominee was also a strong signal by Trump that he was ready to reach an accommodation with party elites, economic conservatism and the religious right. It may well be that Pence played a role in bringing out votes among white evangelicals and overcoming equivocation amongst some about Trump's personality and style.[12] The Pence selection reinforced the belief that Trump could act as 'protector' who would reach out to religious communities who were, in their own eyes, culturally and politically under siege.

In sum, Trump's thinking can be described as a process of *bricolage* insofar as it innovatively recombined and reconfigured older ideas although they were also tied together with newer notions and an array of 'post-truths'. *Bricolage* does not mean that there was a structured, planned and considered process or that the ideas on which the Trump campaign drew were a stable or durable mix. Indeed, there is often profound instability and incoherence as different and competing ideas are brought together: 'the sets of ideas used in bricolage do not necessarily fit together in any coherent way. Often, ideas contain elements of meaning that may conflict with other elements in the idea' (Carstensen, 2011: 156).

His ideas were therefore far from static. Trump seemed to emphasise mainstream Republican claims and policies rather more as the general election campaign progressed. This may have been because his campaign had to reach a *modus vivendi* with some of the Republican Party's elites. Just as a matter of practicalities, it depended upon the Republican National Committee (RNC) and Reince Priebus, its chairman, for resources and in particular its capacity to undertake get-out-the-vote operations.

Trump's Gettysburg address

The speech delivered by Trump at Gettysburg in October 2016 (seemingly a bid to invoke the spirit of Abraham Lincoln) was perhaps the fullest statement of policy that Trump offered and comes close to serving as a campaign manifesto. It illustrates the processes of *bricolage* and the ways in which the campaign's discourses were pulled between populism, strongman politics, paleo-conservative ideas nested within populism, and mainstream Republicanism.

In parts of the speech, setting out the steps that would be taken in the first hundred days of a Trump presidency (which although commonplace as a strategy was itself a way of conveying a strongman theme), he reproduced some of the themes and rallying cries that had defined conservatism and Republicanism since the 1990s. Trump's embrace of these has led some to question the depth or sincerity of his populist credentials. There was a commitment to dramatic tax reductions and to extend the market within education. The speech promised a 'Middle Class Tax Relief and Simplification Act' through which a middle-class family with two children would be given a 35 per cent tax reduction, the number of tax brackets cut from seven to three, and business rates lowered from 35 to 15 per cent. Calculations by the Tax Policy Center suggested that Trump's plans would give a 0.8 per cent tax cut to the bottom 20 per cent of income earners while offering a cut of 50.8 per cent to the top 1 per cent (Rattner, 2017).

The Trump campaign drew upon supply-side economics and perhaps the tax reform proposals put forward by Congressman Paul Ryan, Speaker of the US House of Representatives, to assert that tax reductions would act as a spur to economic activity. Thus, the campaign promised that the reductions, when taken together with other measures including regulatory relief and the lifting of the restrictions on the energy sector, would lead to an annual economic growth rate of 4 per cent and the creation of at least 25 million new jobs. Trump's economic adviser, Stephen Moore, particularly emphasised the supply-side effects that would be generated by the corporate tax reductions:

> The heart of the Trump tax plan is to cut our business tax from the highest in the world down to 15 percent, making our rate one of the lowest. This will reverse the stampede of businesses fleeing out of America – great companies like Burger King and Medtronics. When the businesses come back, so will good paying middle class jobs. (Moore, 2016)

The speech also incorporated proposals for a 'School Choice And Education Opportunity Act' that would create a quasi-market by providing federal funding for school choice projects (perhaps through vouchers) while at the same time ending 'common core' which set national goals for the K-12 curriculum and had been fiercely resented by the right as an attack upon state prerogatives. All of this was well-trodden conservative ground.

At the same time Trump also echoed the fierce opposition to almost every aspect of the Obama presidency that had been absorbed into Republican and conservative thinking during the preceding eight years. Although there were some lacunae and ambiguities in the commitments he gave, Trump said that he would, on becoming president, 'cancel every unconstitutional executive action, memorandum and order issued by President Obama'. A Trump White House would pursue an 'America First energy plan', ease regulatory provisions governing the energy sector, encourage the use of shale, oil, natural gas and 'clean coal', and allow projects such as the Keystone Pipeline to progress. The payments to United Nations climate change programmes would be stopped. A Trump administration would also, he announced, ensure that Supreme Court Justice Antonin Scalia (who had died suddenly in February 2016), would be replaced by a judge who was, like Scalia, a solid conservative. Such a nominee would uphold originalist forms of jurisprudence and maintain a right-wing majority on the Court. Trump offered a list of twenty-one candidates (including Utah Senator Mike Lee) who he said might be nominated to take up the seat.

Trump's address at Gettysburg committed an administration that he would head to the repeal and replacement of the 2010 Patient Protection and Affordable Care Act, which had been the focal point for the Tea Party movement and conservative protests in and out of Congress. 'Obamacare' would, the Gettysburg speech pledged, be replaced by personal Health Savings Accounts, the right to purchase health insurance across state lines, and give the states responsibility for the funds provided to Medicaid (the residual health programme for low-income groupings).

In addition the speech echoed or built upon some of the calls and demands that formed the 1994 *Contract with America* that Congressional Republicans had drafted and signed as a form of platform as part of their campaign to win that year's mid-term elections. They called for a constitutional amendment permitting the imposition of term limits on Congress (a measure inspired by notions of a *citizen legislature*); a requirement that for every new federal regulation that was introduced, two existing regulations should be removed; and a hiring freeze on all federal employees (except those in the armed forces, public safety and public health) so as 'to reduce the federal workforce through attrition'.

The speech also threw out some newer ideas aimed at groupings and constituencies regarded as pivotal in the coming election. For example, the Affordable Childcare and Eldercare Act would permit families to deduct childcare provision and care for the elderly in their tax returns. The American Energy and Infrastructure Act would encourage the creation of public-private partnerships and offer tax incentives so as to trigger large-scale ($1 trillion) infrastructural investment over a ten-year period, a proposal that at face value is more often associated with the left than the right.[13]

Nonetheless, in overall terms, the speech was weighted towards the populism and economic nationalism that had been the defining hallmark of the Trump campaign. The Clean up Corruption in Washington Act offered the promise of reforms to curb the activities of lobbyists so as 'to Drain the Swamp and reduce the corrupting influence of special interests on our politics'. There were to be also measures addressing the trade issue marking a very sharp break with the trade liberalisation policies that the overwhelming majority of elected Republicans had pursued since about 1970. NAFTA would be renegotiated and if this failed the US would withdraw. The US would also pull out from the Trans-Pacific Partnership and China would be labelled a currency manipulator. Alongside this, the End the Offshoring Act would impose tariffs (a figure of 35 per cent was mooted) so as to deter firms from relocating overseas. As president, Trump would furthermore, 'direct the Secretary of Commerce and U.S. Trade Representative to identify all foreign trading abuses that unfairly impact American workers and direct them to use every tool under American and international law to end those abuses immediately' (Murdock, 2016).

And, although Mitt Romney's 2012 presidential campaign had also pledged to pursue illegal immigration (talking of measures that would encourage 'self-deportation'), the prospect of deportation now moved centre-stage. Two million criminal illegal immigrants were to be removed and immigration from 'terror-prone regions' was to be suspended. Immigrants would also be subject to 'extreme vetting'. Even more importantly, there was a reaffirmation of the commitment to construct a wall on the Mexican border and an insistence that the Mexican government would be required to reimburse the full cost (Murdock, 2016).

Ideas and processes of interpretation

Nonetheless, although the Trump campaign can be seen in terms of strategic skill, ideational entrepreneurship and *bricolage* as it reconfigured policy ideas, a note of caution should be sounded. Ideas (including those that drove the Trump campaign) do not exist, and cannot be 'sold', in a vacuum. They are not free-floating. There are certainly processes of interpretation as actors make sense of events, processes and structures but interpretive processes take place within certain bounds. Although there will always be outliers, and flailing election candidates will, for example, vehemently deny the likelihood of an impending defeat, there are limits beyond which interpretation generally does not go.

In his discussion of frames, and the ways in which the Republicans captured issues by capturing the ideas and language within which issues such as taxation are debated, George Lakoff emphasises that frames and the slogans to which they are often tied can only be effectively marketed if the ideas on which they draw have taken root over decades (Lakoff, 2014: 33). Arguably, however, more is required than this. Even the most proficient ideational entrepreneur can only develop, distil and promote policy ideas within certain sets of material circumstances that will viably lend credence to those ideas. There are power relationships and logics that are certainly subject to processes of interpretation but nonetheless operate so as to privilege some ideas rather than others. Economic restructuring, the financial crisis, and the prolonged malaise that followed brought populist frames and fears of downward intergenerational mobility to the fore. And, as Matt Bai has argued, economic issues blurred together with a profound distrust of, and alienation from, governing institutions. This was, Bai suggests, a legacy of the Iraq war, the untruths that accompanied it, and the failure of the US to bring about the form of 'regime change' that had been promised:

> A decade passed, and American voters seemed to have settled into their cynicism ... But politics is like that. The larger the shock to the system, the longer it takes for the effects to surface ... And so, right from the start, he was willing to trash the powerful institutions of our civic life ... Generals were stupid. Judges were biased by their ethnicity. Bankers were venal. His own party was weak and pathetic. (Bai, 2016)

The seeping effects of the Iraq war that Bai describes should be added together with the longer-term ideas that have been fostered and facilitated by the structural characteristics of the American state that were considered in Chapter 2. In sum, ideas should be understood within the context of the 'material' factors considered in the chapters that follow. They only take shape and come to the fore in certain circumstances.

Notes

1 It may also be that Trump's wilder claims and promises were disregarded because many voters were looking for strong leadership and direction rather than specific policy pledges. See p. 44.

2 In September 2016 Trump announced that Barack Obama was in fact, and despite his earlier claims, born in the United States. Trump went on to assert that he had brought the issue to a close.

3 Much of this recalls Richard Hofstadter's celebrated critique of the 'paranoid style' in US politics (Hofstadter, 1996: orig. 1963: 25–26).

4 Arguably, Trump's verbal assaults on finance capital and globalism were framed and bolstered by Bernie Sanders's repeated claims during the primary season that Clinton was very closely tied to Wall Street.

5 Ideational entrepreneurship has been formally defined: '... the political entrepreneur is the political actor who alters the equilibrium of the political market by introducing innovation and by gaining added value from such, often after building new political coalitions in order to challenge the status quo' (Capano and Galanti, 2015: 6)

6 There have also been claims that the Trump campaign was boosted by the planting of false stories that subsequently went viral on Facebook and other social media outlets. The social media seemed to lend themselves to a 'post-truth' regime partly because gatekeepers are largely absent. It may also be that the algorithms used by Facebook or for example Google are

structured so as to reinforce already set opinions. It should, however, be noted that the process of planting false stories was not entirely one-sided and some inflammatory statements were wrongly attributed to Trump by his opponents.

7 The feasibility of Trump's pledge to restore manufacturing jobs was challenged. As a Brookings Institution report noted, productivity advances since the early 1980s dramatically reduced the manufacturing sector's capacity to create large-scale employment (Muro and Liu, 2016).

8 It has been argued the paleo-conservative focus upon an American identity structured around those descended from white Europeans was not only an assault upon Hispanics, African-Americans and Asian-Americans but was also anti-Semitic. Certainly, paleo references to the 'Jewish lobby' seemed to support these claims.

9 Paleo-conservative suspicions of Britain can be seen in, for example, Patrick Buchanan's book, *Churchill, Hitler And 'The Unnecessary War'* which argued that Europe had been plunged into conflict because of British ambitions and miscalculations (Buchanan, 2008).

10 There is a direct connection between paleo-conservatism and the Alt-Right. Paul Gottfried, a paleo stalwart, addressed the H.L. Mencken Club's Annual Meeting in November 2008 and talked of a new generation 'postpaleos' which he referred to as an 'alternative right' (Gottfried, 2016). Congressman Ron Paul's bids to win the Republican presidential nomination proved to be a further rallying point and some of Paul's activists appear to have moved across to Trump in 2016.

11 In 1999, Trump had reportedly said in response to a question about abortion: 'I'm very pro-choice' (quoted in Judis, 2016: 65).

12 Mike Pence was raised as a Roman Catholic but later moved towards and embraced the evangelical megachurches (Mahler and Johnson, 2016).

13 It should be noted, however, that Trump's infrastructure plan was criticised as a proposal to grant extensive tax concessions to the utility industry and construction sector industries (Klain, 2016).

4

Voters

> You could put half of Trump's supporters into what I call the basket of deplorables. Right? The racist, sexist, homophobic, xenophobic, Islamophobic – you name it ... He has given voice to their websites that used to only have 11,000 people – now 11 million. He tweets and retweets their offensive, hateful, mean-spirited rhetoric. Now some of those folks – they are irredeemable, but thankfully they are not America. (Hillary Clinton, September 9th 2016, quoted in Blow, 2016b)

THESE words were thrown back at Hillary Clinton. But who – alongside the 'deplorables' – voted for Trump in the Republican primaries and then in the November election? Which groupings formed the Trump electorate? This chapter considers the shifts and swings amongst voters and suggests that these, alongside ideas about the state and the 'entrepreneurial' efforts of the campaign, form part of the explanation for Trump's eventual victory.

Whatever their limits and flaws, the exit polls provide the most helpful starting point for a discussion. The results were speedily tabulated using a very broad range of categories. They reveal that the Trump electorate was significantly more male (53 per cent of men supported Trump) than female (42 per cent) (CNN Politics, 2016.) Nonetheless, despite forecasts that Trump's personal conduct and style would alienate many women and earlier polling reports which had pointed to big gender-based differences, the gender gap was not significantly bigger at 11 per cent than that seen in presidential contests since 1980. Indeed, according to Pew polling, it had been 10 per cent in 2012

(Chaturvedi, 2016). Trump also won the backing of older age groupings (those aged 45 or above) and those in any but the lowest income groupings (in other words he secured backing from those earning $50,000 or more annually).

Other exit poll categories can be added and reveal patterns. Like preceding Republican presidential candidates, Trump secured majority support from the frequent churchgoers, Protestants (most particularly white evangelicals or 'born-agains'), Mormons and Catholics as well as those who were married, although to some extent marital status is always a function of age. Mobility also mattered. Those white voters who still lived in the community in which they had been raised as a child or lived within a two-hour drive from their original hometown strongly backed Trump (Cox and Jones, 2016). Alongside all of this, there were signs of an urban–rural divide, perhaps overlain by the resentments of those in 'flyover states' against the east and west coasts. Some 62 per cent of those supporting Trump were from rural areas, leading some commentators to claim that this cleavage was *the* story of the election (CNN Politics, 2016).

The importance of the urban–rural divide should not be underestimated. There is a sense that rural areas are neglected by policymakers, they secure relatively few resources, and have distinct values that those in the cities do not understand or respect (Cramer, 2016: 12). Nonetheless, although a plethora of categories can be cited (and the same individuals of course occupy multiple identities at the same time and are therefore to be found in a number of categories) the 2016 exit polls were structured by two absolutely core but related variables. First and foremost, race and ethnicity was paramount. While 58 per cent of whites voted for Trump, 74 per cent of non-whites supported Clinton. This cuts across almost everything else and largely explains the results in many other categories. A majority of white women (53 per cent) supported Trump. More white young people, aged 18–29, backed him (48 per cent) than Clinton (43 per cent). Second, within the prism of race and ethnicity, education attainment levels were pivotal. Although Trump also gained backing from a very large plurality (49 per cent) of white graduates, the figure was much higher (67 per cent) among more than two-thirds of whites without a college degree. White women with a college degree narrowly supported Clinton (51 per cent), and 62 per cent of white women without a college degree backed Trump (CNN Politics, 2016).

What happened? What was going on? Why do these numbers matter so much? Overall turnout declined, falling back to an estimated 55.4 per cent of the voting-age population (VAP) (Wallace and Yoon, 2016). This appears to be the lowest turnout rate since 2000. Nonetheless, although questions have been asked about the findings, exit poll data suggest that while overall turnout fell, there were *not* large demographic differences between those who voted in 2016 and those who had voted in 2012. Indeed, whites constituted a slightly smaller proportion of the voters, their overall share falling from 72 per cent to 70 per cent. All other things being equal, this should have boosted the Democratic ticket's chances.

Furthermore, the exit polls suggest that the overall proportion of white voters supporting the Republican presidential candidate was 58 per cent, more or less the same as in 2012 although that having been said there may have been shifts in the structure and direction of the minority vote. It appears that there was a slight fall in the proportion of African-American voters (the constituency that gives the highest levels of backing to Democratic candidates) and, as a corollary, a slight increase in the proportions of Hispanic and Asian-American voters. More importantly, while some of the figures have been fiercely contested, and although Hillary Clinton still won very large majorities amongst the minority electorate, the exit polls suggest some significant swings to the Republicans among minorities when set against the 2012 presidential election (CNN Politics, 2016).

Nonetheless, although the shift to the Republican ticket was relatively large in proportional terms, these changes in the structure of the minority vote only provide a small part of the overall reason for Trump's victory. Shifts in the social composition of the white Republican vote between 2012 and 2016 were far more important in terms of explaining Trump's victory. Although there was a 10 per cent swing to the Democrats among whites with a college education who may well have found themselves unable to back Trump's candidacy, there was a *14 per cent swing* to the Republicans among those whites who had not had a college education (Huang, Jacoby, Lai and Strickland, 2016).[1]

This shift in the class character of the Republican vote had massive distributional and thus electoral consequences. It gave Trump his victory. This is because states have very different occupational structures and the white population is therefore very different in character. In some states, such as Virginia where Trump was easily defeated, the proportion of whites with a college education and those without is more or less the same. However in other states, working-class whites heavily outnumber those with a college education. This is particularly evident in the states where the manufacturing and extractive industries were formerly concentrated and which now face sustained economic difficulties. In Ohio, for example, there are almost twice as many working-class whites in the electorate when set against those with a college education. The same is true in Wisconsin and Michigan (Bycoffe and Wasserman, 2016). Furthermore, although these are not states with the very highest proportion of whites, there are still very substantial white populations and the minority vote was outnumbered.[2]

There is a further step in the argument. As has been widely noted, Clinton won the popular vote across the country by a significant margin. Nonetheless, because the electoral system is structured around the Electoral College and nearly all states assign all their Electoral Votes to the winner of popular vote on a plurality basis, the shift in the class character of the Republican vote put significant numbers of states into Donald Trump's hands. Indeed, the numbers were sufficient to give him the presidency.

The fate of the Clinton 'firewall'

The states that proved decisive were, therefore, those where there were large numbers of white working-class people when set against those in the higher educational categories. States such as Michigan, Wisconsin and Pennsylvania thereby proved decisive. These were among the states that had been regarded before the election as Hillary Clinton's 'firewall'. If, it was said, she lost swing states such as Florida and Ohio, she would *still* win the presidency because of the Electoral Votes from the firewall states that had long voted for Democratic candidates. Although there were fears in the Clinton camp about Pennsylvania, the other 'firewall' states were more or less taken for granted. Michigan had not voted Republican since 1988 and Wisconsin since 1984. (It should also be added that Pennsylvania had not cast its Electoral Votes for a Republican nominee since 1988). Indeed, Clinton did not visit Wisconsin after becoming the Democratic presidential nominee and there was bemused puzzlement that Trump was campaigning in such solidly blue states. With hindsight, it is worth noting the prescience of *The New Yorker* which, just ahead of Election Day, asked and rightly answered the question 'Why is Donald Trump in Michigan and Wisconsin?' (Cassidy, 2016). He had sensed and was capitalising upon a regional revolt (McQuarrie, 2016).

Thus, the firewall collapsed. Trump's ability to build upon and add to Mitt Romney's results in 2012 by quite spectacularly winning Michigan, Wisconsin and Pennsylvania (as well as states such as Iowa, Indiana and Ohio) gave him the Electoral Votes that he needed for overall victory. Given that the core of Trump's victory and Clinton's defeat lay in the disintegration of the firewall, it is difficult to dissent from claims that the effects of globalising processes and severe economic hardship in these 'Rust Belt' states accelerated defections amongst the ranks of Democratic voters or infrequent voters who might in past elections have voted for the Democratic ticket.[3] In Michigan, real wages in manufacturing fell by 27 per cent between 2003 and 2016. The state lost a third of its manufacturing jobs between the beginning of 2000 and October 2016. Much the same can be said about Ohio, Pennsylvania, Indiana and Wisconsin (Rattner, 2017). A county-by-county analysis of the election results confirms the importance of economic variables. It indicated that Trump performed more strongly in counties where there have been manufacturing losses and as a corollary performed worse where there had been manufacturing gains (Collingwood, 2016).

Macomb County, Michigan, appears representative of Rust Belt politics. It has been much studied and was the basis for the celebrated survey of 'Reagan Democrats' in the 1980s by Stan Greenberg, one of Bill Clinton's key polling advisers. Greenberg recorded the ways in which white, unionised auto workers had been won, at least at that point in presidential contests, to the Republican ticket. They saw the Democrats as increasingly the party of minorities and the undeserving poor. They 'found that these working-class whites interpreted Democratic calls for economic fairness as code for transfer payments to African-Americans' (Greenberg, 2008). By 2008, however, there appeared to have been a sea-change. According to Greenberg, Macomb County had become ' ... normal and uninteresting ... more tolerant and culturally liberal ... '. Obama secured 60 per cent backing. The appearance of 'normality' was however illlusory: 'Not only did Trump win 54 percent of the vote there, but he did so on record high turnout. Without his strength there, he would not be ahead in Michigan by 13,000 votes' (Hohmann, 2016).

Seen in this way, there is thus a fairly direct connection between the 2008 financial crisis, the 'Great Recession', the prolonged malaise that followed and the 2016 election outcome although the polarising effects of some Obama reforms and the Tea Party movement's mobilising efforts should not be underestimated. While US growth rates were higher than those in many European countries they remained tepid. Indeed, according to the Bureau of Economic Analysis the period between 2006 and 2015 was the only ten-year stretch in which the annual inflation-adjusted growth of GDP never reached 3 per cent (Jeffrey, 2016). While recorded unemployment reached a peak of 10 per cent of the labour force in October 2009 and then fell to 4.9 per cent by August 2016 (a figure well below that in many European countries), this hid the substantial numbers who were under-employed, compelled to take jobs at lower wages and in worse conditions or had withdrawn from the labour market (Bureau of Labor Statistics,

2016). Median household income, which had been $57,357 in 2007 was only $53,657 in 2014 (US Census Bureau, 2016).

Furthermore, insofar as there was a recovery from the beginning of 2010 onwards, there was a dramatic divide between those with and those without a college education. The US economy added 11.6 million jobs. Of these, 11.5 million (99 per cent) went to workers with, at the least, some college education (Carnevale, Jayasundera and Gulish, 2016: 1). Just 100,000 jobs, however, went to those who had never attended college. There are thus solid and credible reasons for both the anger that was palpable throughout the election campaign and the demands for radical forms of change.

Although Clinton won a majority amongst those who saw the state of the economy as their number one concern, there was thus an intense thirst for change. According to the exit polls, almost four in ten voters (39 per cent) said that they sought a candidate who could 'bring needed change'. The desire for a candidate who had 'the right experience' was secondary. Among those who wanted change, Trump secured 83 per cent of the popular vote compared with just 14 per cent for Clinton (Cillizza, 2016). Clinton not only represented 'big government' and the status quo, but also the elites that promoted trade liberalisation, financialisation and the politics of the 'new economy' that had so brutally displaced the old.

Processes of interpretation

It might of course be said that if the full picture is considered those who lost out as a consequence of the recession were, to a greater extent, black or Hispanic. Indeed, minorities were in many cases more adversely hit in material terms than whites. And yet, although Latinos did not turn out to vote in the numbers that had been forecast and while greater numbers than expected voted Republican thereby contributing much to Clinton's defeat, they remained solidly committed to the Democratic ticket. At this point, therefore, there is a puzzle that requires explanation.

Why should there be very different political reactions to the economic malaise? One approach would rest theoretically on claims that there are 'logics of calculus' or 'logics of appropriateness' through which actors respond to the circumstances in which they find themselves (Hay, 2011: 66). Thus, events and the institutional arrangements through which they are mediated shape sets of incentives and disincentives or influence norms so as to produce particular perceptions and responses. Thus, it might be argued that minorities failed to turn out or respond in sufficient numbers in support of Clinton because they were substantially more disadvantaged than whites and Clinton failed through what might be termed a 'low energy' campaign to mobilise potential supporters in the same way as Obama in 2008 and 2012.

However, circumstances, settings and institutions do not 'come with a script'. Indeed, they are riddled with ambiguities and uncertainties and they are open to different perceptions and understandings. Given this, processes of interpretation and constructions of self-interest are pivotal. Having said this, and as was noted in Chapter 2, interpretation is not a free-floating process. It does not simply depend upon the energies of ideational entrepreneurs or what has been termed 'strategic conduct'. There are instead bounds beyond which interpretations generally will not go. Because of collective experiences in past decades, African-Americans, Hispanics, Asian-Americans and college-educated women tend to identify their interests with economic interventionism and the expansion of federal social provision. This thus draws them towards the Democratic Party although, having said that, African-American turnout dipped and while Hispanic and Asian-American turnout increased, minority voters failed to give Clinton the level of support that Obama had secured in 2008 and 2012 (CNN Politics, 2016).[4] In contrast, whites, particularly working-class whites, increasingly identified with Republicanism and embraced the economic and cultural themes that defined the Trump campaign. They constructed a notion of interest based upon restricting trade and immigration, toughness towards foreign and domestic enemies, strong leadership, opposition to the Washington 'establishment' and hostility to 'political correctness'.

The last phrase was repeatedly used in media interviews with Trump voters. And Trump exploited the issue. A commentary on the early Republican primaries suggested that:

> Trump has indeed tapped into a deeply felt loathing of 'political correctness,' but his willingness to defy it is larger than his particular statements – it's served to establish his *character* in voters' eyes. It's given him a badge of honor that sets him apart from all his rivals and proves his trustworthiness. (Prokop, 2016b)[5]

Although never defined, 'correctness' appeared to mean a sense that it was inappropriate to use denigrating terms to describe groups or individuals. The interviewees said that they sought the freedom to do just that. Furthermore, it should be said that for many working-class whites (and perhaps whites much more broadly) it seemed that Democratic candidates and legislators had few connections with them. Indeed, the coalitional bloc around which the Democratic Party was built seemed to increasingly rest upon white cultural elites based in the East and West Coast states and the minority vote. It was a coalitional bloc with which relatively few working-class whites could identify.

Warning signs

With hindsight, it is clear that there were warning signs for the Democrats earlier in the year during the primaries. In Ohio, a core Rust Belt state, 14 per cent of those who had been registered Democratic primary voters in 2012 participated in the Republican primary. The figures were higher in some parts of the Buckeye State. In Mahoning County, which is 80 per cent white and in the heart of the Rust Belt, 22.1 per cent of 2012 Democrats cast a ballot in the 2016 Republican race (Sevastopulo, 2016). Alongside reports of this type there were other telltale signs in the primaries that should have provided a warning for those decrying Trump. If his votes in the Republican primaries are considered, RAND Corporation surveys suggest that political efficacy seems to have been highly significant. Those who agreed with the statement 'people like me don't have any say about what the government does' were 86.5 per cent more likely to prefer Trump to his rivals for the nomination (Pollard and Mendelsohn, 2016).

It could also be argued that there were warning signs in earlier presidential elections. In the 2000 presidential election, West Virginia, a solidly white working-class state that had customarily been in the Democratic camp, flipped to the Republicans and backed George W. Bush, thereby handing him the presidency. Nonetheless, because the state had only a handful of Electoral Votes and the belief amongst Democratic commentators that minorities and highly qualified professionals would guarantee a 'coming Democratic majority', West Virginia was written off as an aberration. It was not. There were also hints of what was to come in the other states that gave Trump his victory. In federal elections at least, the Republicans had already become the 'natural' party for white workers in what had been the anthracite belt in Eastern Pennsylvania, the piedmont towns in the Carolinas that were associated with textiles and furniture, and across much of Appalachia (Davis, 2016).

With hindsight, the coalitional bloc around which the contemporary Democratic Party was constructed was much more fragile than it appeared in the years preceding the 2016 elections. Obama's presidential election victories in 2008 and 2012 hid this. Indeed, they allowed left-leaning commentators to rejoice in the belief that there had been a process of realignment, based upon the growing weight of minorities and qualified professionals within the electorate, through which the Democrats had secured a stable and enduring majority. From this perspective, the Democrats could look forward to a prolonged period, perhaps decades, as the *hegemonic* party. At times, it appeared in their claims that demography was indeed destiny.[6] All of this, however, diverted attention away from the fragility of the Democratic bloc. While the Democrats were certainly the majority party within the minority electorate, the overwhelming majorities and the high levels of turnout in 2008 and 2012 were in significant part a function of Obama's abilities as a campaigner. And the Republicans continued to capture the white vote, particularly if those without a college education are considered. Despite the magnitude of his 2008 victory, Obama won only 40 per cent of the votes of 'non-college' whites (CNN Politics, 2008).

Europe

Nonetheless, although American populism has had and continues to have some distinctive features, and as noted in Chapter 2 has long been firmly implanted within US political culture, there are pronounced ideational overlaps between Trump's campaign and the contemporary European right-wing populist parties. Viktor Orbán, the Hungarian Prime Minister, was jubilant on hearing the election result, seeing it as another step towards a counter-revolution against migration, multiculturalism, supra-nationalism and efforts to 'export' democracy (Foster, 2016). The role Nigel Farage, the leader of the United Kingdom Independence Party (UKIP), played as a Trump surrogate and supporter during the election campaign has been widely noted. Marine Le Pen, leader of the Front National, talked about her affinities with Trump in terms of foreign policy but there was also, she said, extensive common ground on domestic policy issues such as immigration, the role of the state and collective identity. She hailed his election victory: 'It's the emergence of a new world ... It's the end of the 20th century.' Geert Wilders of the Freedom Party in the Netherlands was even more openly enthusiastic: 'Congratulations! A historic victory! A revolution! We will return our country to the Dutch ... We are witnessing the same uprising on both sides of the Atlantic' (Nossiter, 2016).

Insofar as the Trump vote was a revolt by whites, particularly those with lower levels of education, this is not just a US story. There have of course been comparable processes in much of Europe as globalisation has taken its toll. The story was popularised through the 'elephant graph' depicting changes in real income during the twenty years between 1998 and 2008. Real incomes rose very markedly for all but those at the very bottom of the world income distribution scale and those whose incomes lay between the 75th and 90th percentile (those in the lower half of the income range in the richer countries). For these people there was income stagnation. The curve thus formed roughly the shape of an elephant.

Subsequent studies have suggested that the elephantine character of the curve should be modified significantly. They indicate important cross-national variations (suggesting that factors other than globalisation should be given more attention) and conclude that there may have been some income growth amongst those between the 75th and 90th percentiles although less than amongst other groupings. In loose terms, the original elephant shape remains as a point of reference of analyses (Corlett, 2016: 8).

The failure of globalising processes to deliver the gains for many manual workers in the developed world that they did for others fused together with long-running economic change and the decline of traditional industry to break the ties between the working class, the trades unions and social democratic parties. Social democratic parties (and some other 'mainstream' parties) were increasingly unable to mobilise voters. Party membership and voter identification with these parties declined. Those who had lost out, or perceived themselves to have lost out, from globalising processes felt that their interests were not being addressed, leading to new and different cleavages amongst the voting public (Kriesi and Pappas, 2016: 2–3). Thus, the decline of social democracy led, as a corollary, to the growth of newer populist parties, movements and candidacies.

There are certainly some firm associations between processes of economic change, the state of the economy from 2008 onwards, and the populist surge on both sides of the Atlantic. In Europe, for example, the countries that were hardest hit economically experienced substantial electoral volatility (Kriesi and Pappas, 2016: 14).

'Not the wretched of the earth'

Nonetheless, as has been seen, and although there were large-scale defections among college-educated whites away from the Republican ticket probably as a reaction to the candidate's style, personality and politics, the Trump electorate extended way beyond the ranks of the white working class. After all, as the exit polls showed, Trump won 58 per cent of the total white vote (CNN Politics, 2016).

The inter-class character of his support was evident in the primaries. As was noted: 'Trump's supporters are not the wretched of the earth' (Matthews, 2016). Much more generally, the picture was, as a Norwegian observer noted, much the same in Europe if patterns of support for right populist parties are considered:

> ... they've done well in the richer regions. Think about Italy, where they've done well in the north, or Belgium, where they've done well in the north – or the fact that the populists are in government in my country, Norway, which is [one of the] richest countries on the planet. (quoted in Beauchamp, 2016)

How, therefore, should we explain support from Trump amongst whites within the higher-income and higher educational attainment categories? Trump won a plurality (49 per cent) of the vote amongst white college graduates. Why?

Studies of Rust Belt towns and cities suggest that processes of economic decline did not only hit those on the lowest rungs of the ladder. There is evidence of broader, inter-class resentments about the demise of locally owned industry. Job losses led in turn to the hollowing out of community structures and the erosion of social capital leaving many alienated and resentful (Pacewicz, 2016).

Another part of the answer, but only part and perhaps not that big a part, is tied to gender. In overall terms, 53 per cent of men supported Trump while the figure for women was 42 per cent, thus creating an 11 per cent gender gap. Amongst college graduates, the gender gap was smaller at 9 per cent (54 per cent of men and 45 per cent of women backed Trump). It is tempting to regard this gender gap as a function of Trump's very overtly male tone and seeming disregard for women, an attitude highlighted once the *Access Hollywood* video-recording had been released. It is also always easy to depict populist insurgencies in terms of 'angry white men'. Nonetheless, the overall gender gap has been a constant feature of US electoral politics since at least 1980. It had been, if measured in terms of the proportions of men and women voting Republican, 10 per cent in 2000, 7 per cent in 2004, 5 per cent in 2008 and 8 per cent in 2012. The gap was therefore bigger than that in earlier election years but not exceptionally larger.

Age also matters. Amongst whites, if the different age cohorts are considered, the highest level of support for Trump came from those in the 45–64 age-bracket, 63 per cent of whom backed the Trump campaign.[7] There was a 15 per cent gap between the senior citizens and younger voters aged 18–29. Age has clearly been a factor in the history of recent conservative mobilisations. In their survey of the Tea Party movement Theda Skocpol and Vanessa Williamson pointed to the age profile of activists at a meeting in Ohio:

> graying hairs topped almost every head. Although quite a few of the group leaders we met were women in their forties, the bulk of those in attendance were unmistakably in their fifties, sixties, seventies, and even older. (Skocpol and Williamson, 2012: 25)

Within the Tea Party movement, the politics of those in the older age brackets went beyond the conservatism that sometimes accompanies age. Instead, the movement (and there is every reason to think that this might in part have informed the Trump electorate), was not only moulded by anxieties about illegal immigrants and undeserving 'free-loaders' but also particular representations of the young. They were seen as having a sense of entitlement and dependency. They had, it was said by many of the movement's participants, lost the traditional work ethic (Skocpol and Williamson, 2012: 72–74). However, the 2016 exit polls suggest that this was a racialised phenomenon. There is little evidence of comparable age gaps within the Hispanic and African-American population (CNN Politics, 2016). In sum, race trumps age.

The most convincing explanation is that, to use a phrase employed in the run-up to Election Day, Republicans 'came home'. There had been sustained opposition amongst some Republicans and conservatives to Trump's candidacy. Indeed a 'never Trump' campaign was established within the party's ranks. Commentators such as William Kristol, editor of *The Weekly Standard*, and the humourist P.J. O'Rourke were very critical and Republican elites generally kept Trump at arm's length. Nonetheless, as early voting took place and the election drew near many Republican and Republican-leaning voters clearly decided that, whatever their reservations, criticisms and dislike of Trump they would back him. They may well have been heavily represented among the large numbers (13 per cent) who were late deciders and only came to a conclusion in the final week before Election Day. In the end 90 per cent of voters defining themselves as Republican voted for Trump (fractionally higher than the proportion of Democrats who supported Clinton) (CNN Politics, 2016). Revealingly, even amongst those 'concerned' about the prospect of a Trump victory, 34 per cent cast a vote for him (CNN Politics, 2016).

Why then did Republicans eventually 'come home' and back Trump despite having, in many cases, reservations or indeed strong reservations about him? The innate strength of partisanship is a large part of the answer. While the proportion of the electorate who are strong identifiers is not very high (particularly on the Republican side given that the figure was just 15 per cent in 2012) there are significant numbers if strong and weaker identifiers are added together and considered alongside Republican 'leaners'. These are those who say that they are 'independent' but 'lean' towards the Republicans. The 1992 book, *The Myth of the Independent Voter*, suggested that although many people claim to be independent (probably because it is widely understood as a virtue) only 11 per cent of the electorate are truly neutral (Keith, Magleby, Nelson, Orr, Westlye and Wolfinger, 1992). At the same time, the presidential election posed a binary choice between Trump and Clinton and Clinton constituted a significant 'Other'. A Pew study suggested that a plurality of Trump supporters (33 per cent) supported him because 'he is not Clinton'. This outweighed other considerations including his policy positions and his ability to bring about change. A comment made by a 44 year-old woman was illustrative: 'I don't like him – he seems arrogant and egotistical. That said, he's the lesser of two evils I'm seeing for this year's election. But not by much' (Pew Research Center, 2016a). One anonymous conservative commentator writing in the *Claremont Review of Books* recalled the attacks of September 11th 2001 and dubbed it 'the Flight 93 Election'. The country was, 'Publius Decius Mus' argued, akin to a hijacked plane. Voting for Trump was a desperate move that could be compared with passengers charging the cockpit. The consequences might possibly be disastrous but any other course would certainly prove fatal. Trump offered the only – and probably last – opportunity to redeem a 'corrupt republic' (Sanneh, 2017).

This prompts a further question. Why did large numbers of Republicans (and some independents) intensely dislike or indeed hate Hillary Clinton? Many observations have been made. Some suggest that it is personal. She has been said to lack a personality outside of politics. She allegedly 'talks down' to others. It may be that for many white working-class voters her style recalled the approaches taken by many professionals. And it is professionals that they despise rather than the wealthy. Indeed, the wealthy are admired. Professionals, however, are truly flawed. A commentator notes that her blue-collar father 'could not say the word *doctor* without the virtual prefix *quack*. Lawyers were *shysters* ... and professors were without exception *phonies*'. Teachers were regarded as condescending and unhelpful (Joan Williams, 2016). It may also be that Clinton's pursuit of policy and politics jarred with still widely held understandings of a woman's appropriate style and place. As First Lady, by dint of her personality, Clinton challenged the conventional perceptions of the role. Her comment in the 1992 election campaign summed it up: 'I suppose I could have stayed home and baked cookies'. She then went on to chair the task force that produced the abortive 1993 healthcare reform plan. She could thus easily be represented (and here again there is more than a hint of misogyny) as a Lady Macbeth figure engaged in power-based intrigues while her husband formally occupied the presidency. Indeed, she was during this period the subject of countless conspiracy theories. At the same time there were also many questions about her ethical standards and the alleged pursuit of private gain through, for example, the Clinton Foundation that Trump captured in the epithet 'crooked Hillary'. For many conservatives she had few guiding principles and her beliefs were instead up for sale:

> She is whatever she feels the need to be in the moment: pro- and anti-free trade, anti- and pro-same-sex marriage, anti- and pro-raising the minimum wage, and pro- and anti-drivers licenses for illegal immigrants. (Charen, 2016)

Perhaps, however, her greatest liability was that she was a consummate political insider. As noted above, she personified the 'political class'. She had been involved in Washington politics for more than a quarter of a century as First Lady, Senator and Secretary of State. The US presidential election process, however, often favours those who can represent themselves as outsiders and can thus claim to be untarnished (or largely untarnished) by the elitist deal-making that is said to characterise the nation's capital. Most successful presidential candidates have either been outsiders or able to frame themselves as such. Barack Obama had for example been in the US Senate just two years when he launched his presidential campaign.

Having been an insider for so long, Clinton was closely associated with 'big government' throughout an era when it was seemingly becoming much bigger. While such sentiments may have been illegitimate or unfair, she was too closely associated with bloated and interventionist forms of government, regulation, extended and over-lavish social provision as well as a reckless foreign policy that, it was charged, put Americans in harm's way.

She thus alienated many white Republican leaners, including those with higher educational qualifications, who given all of this overcame their personal distaste and cast a vote for Donald Trump.

Notes

1. A note of caution should of course be sounded. The figures are net flows. Between elections individuals move in and out of the electorate and particular voting blocs.
2. Economic factors may have been compounded by feelings of racial beleaguerement or threat in the face of growing diversity. There is some evidence that Trump's vote was higher in counties where there had been a significant increase in the number of Hispanics since 2000 (Collingwood, 2016). There are also data suggesting that in the eight years preceding the 2016 election, attitudes towards race, and in particular racial resentment, became more strongly correlated with partisan identification. Thus, for example, the belief that whites are treated unfairly compared with minorities was 'an unusually strong predictor of support for Donald Trump' (Tesler, 2016).
3. The 'rustbelt effect' may have also been felt in Florida which tipped towards Trump. Significant numbers of Florida voters formerly lived in the North-East and Upper-Midwest.
4. It may well be that restrictive state laws, seeking to tighten the forms of identification required to cast a vote, played a part in depressing African-American turnout (Brennan Center for Justice, 2016). In 2016, according to the Brennan Center for Social Justice at New York University School of Law, fourteen states had new voting restrictions in place for the first time including strict photo ID requirements. Estimates suggested that 11 per cent of eligible voters lacked one of the forms of photo ID that were generally required under these laws and they were likely to be black, Latino, on a low income, a student or elderly. Furthermore, the exit polls' findings about the character of the Latino vote have been vigorously challenged. Other survey data suggest that Hispanics voted Democratic in greater numbers

than ever before and only 18 per cent backed Trump (Sanchez and Barreto, 2016).

5   Original emphasis.
6   Some, despite the 2016 election result, still retain their faith in the logic of demography. The white working class, they note, is still shrinking as a proportion of the overall electorate. Thus 2016 may prove to be 'the final time that blue-collar whites will determine a national election' (Moser, 2016).
7   If senior citizens are taken together regardless of race or gender, there was a swing (4 per cent) to the Democrats.

5

Sequences

THE book has already surveyed some of the different explanatory frameworks that can be employed to account for Trump's eventual victory. It has considered the populist tradition and the ways in which it was at least in part shaped by the structures of the state, the ideational character of the Trump campaign, the impact of economic malaise and globalising processes upon the white working class, and the deeply felt opposition amongst many Republican voters and 'leaners' to Hillary Clinton who was seen as a divisive 'machine' candidate.

This chapter looks at another line of explanation. It assesses Trump's ascendancy as a function of, and reaction to, the strategies and discourses pursued in the years preceding 2016 by Republican Party elites. Arguably, Trump's victory was the product of a chain reaction. In other words, it may be that Republican elites, through the discourses that they adopted *in pursuit of given electoral logics*, set off particular sets of *reactive sequences* that culminated, over time, in the emergence of the Trump campaign.

The concept of reactive sequences is a form of path dependence. Nonetheless, it differs markedly from the usual representations of path dependence as a process of self-reinforcing sequences through which a policy path becomes increasingly 'sticky' and resistant to radical change over time. Instead, if there is a path structured around reactive sequences, 'each event in the sequence is both a reaction to antecedent events and a cause of subsequent events' (Mahoney, 2000: 526). Thus, early events set 'in motion a chain of tightly linked reactions and counter-reactions' (Mahoney,

2000: 527). The likelihood of counter-reactions is an important feature of path dependence when understood in this form because they might well take the path in a new and different direction rather than bolstering or extending the path established during the initial stages in the process.

The starting point of a path structured around reactive sequences can of course be difficult to identify. Indeed, in some accounts, the process of identification can at times seem rather arbitrary. One can, after all, always go backwards in time. Often, however, at least in historical sociology, the starting point or 'conjuncture' represents the coming together or intersection of at least two or, more probably, several sequences. Contingency comes in at this point insofar as the ways in which they come together was not foreseeable or a simple progression from earlier occurrences (Mahoney, 2000: 527). Although largely used to capture processes of institutional change, the concept of reactive sequences can also be employed to show the ways in which an ideational shift will in turn trigger further shifts or moves. As noted, they may be either reactions or counter-reactions.

How can this be applied to contemporary US politics? Arguably, over recent decades, Republican members of Congress, those who served in state legislatures, and the party's elites increasingly turned to electoral strategies structured around 'base mobilization'. Instead of seeking the median voter, once described as the quest of the rational party, they sought instead to increase levels of electoral turnout amongst core constituencies. Where turnout is, as in the US, relatively low there is 'slack' that can be taken up.

It is difficult to identify a proximate cause for the adoption of this strategy (and its pursuit is rarely acknowledged publicly) and there are different explanations. They are all associated with processes of polarisation (a process that was particularly pronounced on the Republican side of the aisle), and the declining numbers of genuinely independent voters. In the absence of a substantial 'middle ground', strategists turned instead to their core constituencies. New cleavages emerged around, for example, social and cultural issues (most obviously abortion) thereby leading to a more polarised electorate. The emergence of a highly partisan and polarising media through talk-radio, *Fox News*, and an array of internet platforms certainly fuelled the process. A part may also have been played by residential 'sorting' within the electorate as some groups of people increasingly looked for areas to live where they would be placed with those who shared their values and were like-minded (Mann and Ornstein, 2012: 49–50). There was then a process of *value reinforcement* as individuals only moved in their own circles. It may have been the 'hijacking' of the democratic process by activists, advocacy organisations and highly committed partisans who used primaries and, in particular, caucuses and conventions to impose candidates far removed from the centre ground (Fiorina, 2005: 148–154). Another approach would be to point to the efforts of Republican and Democratic partisans in redrawing the boundaries for elections to the US House of Representatives and state legislatures (Carson, Crespin, Finocchiaro and Rohde, 2007). In seats that were safe for their party, candidates did not have to address the middle ground or those who might support a rival party's candidate. Money and campaign advertising have also been a factor. Republican incumbents require campaign contributions from conservative networks and fear that if they compromise or promote bipartisan causes an 'independent' ad campaign will be mounted against them in their district or state (Mann and Ornstein, 2012: 78). Wherever the answer lies, a process was set in motion by which candidates for public office turned to ever more radical forms of rhetoric in bids to impassion sections of the core electorate. In sum, those who constitute the Republican 'base' secured a grip on the party's elected officials and ensured its shift towards the hard right:

> They certify and work for conservative candidates, they keep conservative issues and ideas in the spotlight, and they threaten the politically wayward with excommunication. And so, election by election, the pull of the base grows and the sway of the center declines. (Hacker and Pierson, 2005: 111)

Having said that, the polarisation process was to some degree contained in presidential contests. While most Republican primary seasons were bitterly contested, 'establishment' candidates such as Bob Dole, George W. Bush, John McCain and Mitt Romney eventually won out. Nonetheless, the picture was different in lower-tier elections. There was a marked shift rightwards in the composition of the Republican caucus serving in the House of Representatives although the process of change took longer, amongst Republicans in the Senate. Then, in the 2008 presidential campaign, there was a shift when Senator John McCain, whose bid was flailing badly, sought a 'game change'. His adoption of Alaska Governor Sarah Palin as his vice-presidential running mate, and her quasi-independent election campaign, marked an important turning point. Increasingly, she sought to mobilise support among core constituencies by questioning the legitimacy of Obama's candidacy and his qualifications for office. In its desperation for votes, the McCain campaign gave her licence to represent Obama as 'someone who sees America as imperfect enough to pal around with terrorists who targeted their own country' (quoted in Heilemann and Halperin, 2010: 408).

Looking ahead immediately to the 2010 mid-term contests and the regaining of enduring Congressional majorities, Republican elites then sought, in the wake of the McCain defeat, to block any form of compromise with the Obama White House. Increasingly they framed issues in cataclysmic terms that would mobilise core conservatives. They thus sought to block the passage of legislation and not only acquiesced in, but fanned the flames of the Tea Party movement. The movement, an unstructured network of activists and grassroots groupings as well as elite-sponsored initiatives, which emerged just a month after Obama took office, looked back to the days of the Boston Tea Party, invoked a spirit of rebellion against tyranny, and demanded a return to 'constitutional' government. It directed many of its efforts against the passage of the Affordable Care Act that ushered in 'Obamacare' and represented, for activists, a further stage along t road to 'big government' and tyranny. At its peak in 2011, estimates suggested that Tea Party groupings had a membership of about 160,000 (Judis, 2016: 56). And, for a period at least, the movement secured support far beyond its ranks. An NBC News / *Wall Street Journal* poll at the beginning of 2010 suggested that 41 per cent of Americans had a 'positive view' of the movement. In contrast, just 35 per cent had a positive view of the Democrats and only 28 per cent had a positive view of the Republican Party (Brooks, 2010).

However, the process was not straightforward. All too often, while lending credence and support to the Tea Party movement and activists of the right, the Republican leadership could not deliver on the promises and commitments that it had made. It aroused hopes that could not be fulfilled. In October 2013, efforts by Congressional Republicans to defund and delay Obamacare triggered a government shutdown. In the end, after sixteen days when much of the government had ceased to function, John Boehner, the Republican Speaker of the House of Representatives and some other less hardline Republicans backed down. Some 87 House Republicans and all of the Democrats voted to restore government funding without any concessions of consequence to Obamacare's opponents. The Senate backed the bill by 81 votes to 18. 'Establishment' conservatives such as Karl Rove, President George W. Bush's principal electoral strategist distanced themselves from confrontational strategies:

> The desire to strike at ObamaCare is praiseworthy. But any strategy to repeal, delay or replace the law must have a credible chance of succeeding or affecting broad public opinion positively. The defunding strategy doesn't ... It is an ill-conceived tactic, and Republicans should reject it. (Rove, 2013)

The sequences continued and the fuelling of passions and the dashing of hopes set the scene for a different and more radical insurgency. Trump offered a means by which Tea Party supporters could challenge or perhaps hit back at the Republican 'establishment'. As Joel Aberbach noted: 'the New York businessman was able to present himself as the heir to the Tea Party revolution, which many activists felt had been quashed or betrayed' (quoted in Aberbach, 2017: 132). Seen in this way, Trump was the product of party elites who, at least until his election, largely disowned him.

6

Order, timing and chance

THE preceding chapters have considered some of the reasons why the Trump insurgency proved victorious. Nonetheless, it is important to go further and explain why events unfolded as they did in 2015–2016. After all, the evidence suggests that just a few years earlier, when the Tea Party movement was at its peak, Trump was hardly regarded as a credible political figure. In their study of the movement, Theda Skocpol and Vanessa Williamson record: 'When Donald Trump was blustering about Obama's birth certificate, he got a chuckle and an "Atta boy" from some Tea Partiers, but no one seemed to take him seriously as a presidential contender.' (Skocpol and Williamson, 2012: 194)

Yet Trump succeeded when comparable candidates failed in earlier years. His precursors include, most notably, the former White House adviser and commentator Patrick J. Buchanan, who sought the Republican presidential nomination in both 1992 and 1996.[1] Why therefore did Buchanan's campaigns crash and burn whereas Trump won the White House? Although Buchanan placed greater emphasis upon the 'religious war' than Trump, he often spoke in very similar terms. He called for protectionist measures and, in contrast with the free market hawks, pointed to a role for government in protecting and preserving the American heartlands. Like Trump, he distanced himself from 'neocon' visions of the US's global role, stressing the country's heritage as a republic rather than an empire. Just as there were close affinities between Trump and the 'Alt-Right', there were associations between Buchanan and paleo-conservatism. Yet, Buchanan remained at the margins whilst Trump seized the presidency.

The changed economic context self-evidently provides a part of the answer to this. Buchanan made his pitch against the background of a visibly improving economy. Nonetheless, other factors are also in play. Much comes down to simple chance and contingency. Whereas Buchanan faced President George H.W. Bush alone in 1992 (although it was a fight he could not hope to win) and a field of about half-a-dozen in 1996, there were 17 more or less credible candidates seeking the 2016 Republican presidential nomination. An open contest in a season that might offer a Republican victory and when there was no 'heir apparent' inevitably brings in large numbers. Because of name recognition and his status as a celebrity, Trump had very significant start-up advantages over other 'outsider' candidates such as Dr Ben Carson or Carly Fiorina. He then built, as has been noted, a solid base amongst those who regarded identity and identity-related economic issues such as immigration and trade as pivotal. At the same time, the votes of those who opposed him were split between rival contenders and Trump was implicitly hailed, despite comments and claims that would have killed off any other candidacy, as a victor with the support of only about a third of the voters.

Timing and sequencing and the order in which candidates withdrew from the race then played a part. At the end of the day, Trump was left facing Texas Senator Ted Cruz whose backing was, because of his absolutist positions on both economic and cultural issues, largely confined to those who defined themselves as 'very conservative'. Trump had a broader base insofar as he could also draw on those who were 'somewhat conservative' (Aberbach, 2017: 133). Then, once he had won the Republican nomination, he was pitched against Hillary Clinton who had been wounded by Senator Bernie Sanders's long primary campaign, the email controversy, the handicaps associated with being a long-time Washington insider, her inability to offer any promise of change that could be sold beyond the party's ranks and persistent doubts about her 'trustworthiness'.

Even at the end of the campaign, there were chance events that probably further damaged Clinton's chances of victory. Just ten days ahead of Election Day, FBI Director James Comey wrote to Congress stating that further emails relevant to earlier investigations of Clinton's emails had been uncovered. Although later rowed back, the damage was done. There have also been suggestions that, as in the 2000 presidential election, small numbers of votes for minor party candidates, and the Greens' Jill Stein and Gary Johnson, the Libertarian candidate, may have prevented the Democratic ticket from winning some states. Nonetheless, this should not be overstated. Even if it is assumed that that all these votes would have been given to Clinton had these candidates not stood (an improbable claim at least in Johnson's case), analysis suggests it is likely that she would still have lost (Golshan, 2016).

Notes

1   Buchanan also stood as the Reform Party candidate in the November 2000 presidential election, attracting 0.4% of the popular vote. At one point, Trump also sought the party's nomination and, after he had withdrawn, condemned Buchanan's racist associations.

7

Afterword: Donald Trump, neoliberalism and political reconfiguration

THERE are further questions that should now be asked. What are the likely consequences of Trump's victory? What are the implications of the 2016 presidential election and its outcome for political and economic processes? Answers to these questions require context. Studies of the period from the time of the 2008 financial crisis onwards have taken the concept of *neoliberalism* as their starting point. Although there are definitional problems and the term is less widely used in the US than in Europe, it captures the changes wrought from the late 1970s onwards and ways in which the post-war Keynesian settlement was dismantled through deregulation, privatisation and the pulling back of state social provision. In broad terms, and although there were very significant differences between countries as neoliberalism took 'embedded' or 'hybrid' forms, the neoliberal agenda (expressed in most notably the Washington Consensus) rested upon the squeezing of the social state, fiscal discipline, the curbing of government subsidies, the cutting of tax rates to bolster trade and financial liberalisation, privatisation, deregulation and the consolidation of property rights (Williamson, 2004: 3–4). To this might be added the 'benchmarking' of relationships on the basis of market competitiveness and the belief that policies should only be adopted if they won the confidence of the financial markets (Ban, 2016). There were of course all sorts of exceptions or deviations from these 'rules' (fiscal discipline was often more honoured in the breach than in the observance) but they remained broad goals.

More than this, neoliberalisation (and here it moved beyond classical nineteenth-century liberalism) held up the promise of globalising processes. From this perspective, intensified cross-border interactions and resource flows would as a corollary lessen the importance of nation-states. Some even said the nation would be no more. In its place, there was a focus on ways of enlarging the scope and capacity of supra-national institutions.

Neoliberalisation expressed itself in other parallel ways. Social class but also gender and race seemed to be losing their importance as definitional categories. Old prejudices, which for some had been the building blocks or order, were being discarded. Instead, as Michel Foucault memorably put it, individuals were all becoming entrepreneurs. *Homo Economicus* is an 'entrepreneur of himself, being for himself his own capital, being for himself his own producer, being for himself the source of (his) earnings' (Foucault, 2010: 226). In this neoliberal vision, the marketplace is open to all comers and for it to function as it should there has to be mobility of capital, labour, goods and services. The barriers, constraints and prejudices of the past no longer have a place.

As neoliberalisation took hold, there was a giddy optimism. The freeing up of markets appeared to offer visible economic benefits and rewards. Even critics conceded that there were creative opportunities (Hall and Lamont, 2013: 2). More importantly, the extreme business cycle fluctuations of earlier years had been ameliorated and there was talk of a 'Great Moderation' from the mid-1980s onwards. The avoidance of a recession in 2000–2001 when the new technology boom came to an end and the shock of the 9/11 attacks appeared to provide further testimony for those who believed that economic processes had been transformed and the excesses of the market had been tamed.

The shock of the financial crisis and the 'Great Recession' cannot be overstated. It triggered an immediate wave of commentaries suggesting that the neoliberal era had reached its conclusion. In October 2008, a German publisher reported that it had just sold 1,500 copies of *Das Kapital* compared to its customary annual average of about 200. The firm's director said:

'It's definitely in vogue right now ... the financial crisis brought us a huge bump' (*BBC News*, 2008). Eleven months later, there were still claims suggesting that neoliberalism had expired but this time around, its place had been taken not by Marxism but, as the title of Robert Skidelsky's book put it, by 'the return of the master'. The 'master' in question was of course John Maynard Keynes. The developed countries had been, it was said, compelled by the severity of the crisis to return to government economic management and, in particular, the use of pro-active fiscal policy (Skidelsky, 2009).

Nonetheless, despite proclamations announcing the death of neoliberalism it not only survived but emerged reinvigorated just two years later. From 2010–2011 onwards, governments had the confidence to abandon 'emergency Keynesianism' and embark upon *austerity* programmes designed to reduce the scale and scope of government expenditure. In some instances, this went beyond a commitment to shrink the budget deficits that had ballooned as the recession took its economic toll. In the UK, David Cameron began talking of a commitment to a permanently 'leaner, more efficient state' (Ashbee, 2015: 128). At the same time, alongside these efforts to reconfigure the state, technological advances bolstered neoliberalisation as the 'gig economy' (most obviously Uber) began to turn a proportion of the labour force into the entrepreneurs of which Foucault spoke.

In the US, after an initial expansionary period, the federal government budget sequester, endorsed by both Republicans and Democrats, accelerated a process of deficit reduction that was at times faster and sharper than that taking place in the UK and certainly continental Europe. Monetary policies also had a neoliberal twist. In place of fiscal policy, the US Federal Reserve and other central banks not only kept interest rates at a minimum for very prolonged periods but stepped into the breach and embarked upon quantitative easing (QE) programmes. While these may have rescued countries from the economic abyss, they also bolstered stock prices, fuelled asset bubbles and thereby increased inequalities. The US Gini coefficient, the principal measure of equality and inequality, rose from 0.376 on the eve of the financial crisis in 2007 to 0.389 in 2012 (Organisation for Economic Co-operation and Development, 2016). Real median wages only recovered from the recession at a very slow rate. Life for the 'precariat' became yet more fragile.

Against the background of these developments and trends, commentators hailed the survival and perhaps rebirth of neoliberalism. Why, it was asked, had alternative paradigms failed to establish themselves? How had austerity been imposed with seeming political ease? Why did the banking sector, seen by most although not all as the source of the financial crisis, emerge more or less unscathed?

> The crisis challenged the foundation stones of the long-dominant neoliberal ideology but it seemed to emerge largely unscathed. The banks were bailed out; hardly any bankers on either side of the Atlantic were prosecuted for their crimes; and the price of their behaviour was duly paid by the taxpayer. (Jacques, 2016)

Nonetheless, there is a very important paradox. Whereas neoliberalism survived economically, and for the most part elites maintained their position, some of its political underpinnings were subject to increasing strain. For decades, neoliberalism has been politically upheld, extended or ameliorated by established 'mainstream' parties. In the US and UK, the rule of the right gave way to 'new' Democrats and Labour, both of which embraced and in some instances extended many of the neoliberal reforms enacted during the preceding decade. There were then twists and turns as sections of the right won electoral victories on the basis of 'compassionate conservatism' and the promise of a 'Big Society'.

Those long-established parties have now, as the crisis has taken its toll, come under substantial strain. Processes of 'party decline' have accelerated. Perhaps more importantly, in Europe at least, new parties have emerged and parties once associated with the fringes and promising much more illiberal forms of democracy have become institutionalised. As a 2016 report surveying both right- and left-wing European populism and published by

Timbro, the Swedish free market think-tank, caught the scale of the change:

> Today, populist parties are represented in the governments of nine European countries and act as parliamentary support in another two. Hence, one third of the governments of Europe are constituted by or dependent on populist parties ... taken together, this wave constitutes the biggest change in the European political landscape at least since the fall of the Berlin Wall (Heinö, 2016: 4).

In the US, because party structures are much more porous and pliable, the populist surge was channelled through a two-party system and, given Trump's primary victories, the pressures were felt most immediately and acutely within the Republican Party. Established conservative currents were brutally disrupted. There were also class divisions that added to the tensions within Republican ranks. The Trump campaign captured much of the working-class support for Republicanism and divided it from the elites that had hitherto maintained a hold over the party's direction: 'What Donald Trump has identified is a party that is literally splitting apart between the donor class and the working class parts of the party' (Caldwell and Sarlin, 2016). During the election campaign, the party's elites were compelled to choose between distancing themselves from Trump, acquiescing in his candidacy, or pursuing some form of uneasy neutrality. Once he had won, they uneasily embraced him.

In both its European and American forms, right-wing populism put the nation, class, race and the role of the state back on the agenda. In doing so it was capturing and building upon shifts that had been evident for some years. In the US, references to a 'working class' had been few and far between long before the advent of the neoliberal era. In most discourses, almost everyone was subsumed within the American 'middle class'. Yet, under the weight of the crisis class made a re-appearance. According to Gallup polling in the US, only 33 per cent called themselves working class in 2000 but by 2015 the figure had risen to 48 per cent (Jacques, 2016). The Trump campaign, which explicitly identified with the blue-collar working class and promised the restoration of traditional industries in the Rust Belt states, was therefore tapping into shifting understandings of class positions. As Trump stated:

> We're going to get those miners back to work ... the miners of West Virginia and Pennsylvania, which was so great to me last week, Ohio and all over are going to start to work again, believe me. They are going to be proud again to be miners (quoted in Worstall, 2016).

Nonetheless, Trump and contemporary populism did not draw on or employ social class in a 'pure' form or in ways that ape those pursued by the radical left. Instead, just as the 'people' is understood in particular ways, populist understandings of class are based upon particular class *fractions*. Trump's working class, and the same can be said of the European populist parties, is largely male (although some polling suggests that his support may actually be higher among some groups of women than men) and is very largely white.[1] Working-class interest is then fused with the resurrection of the nation (that neoliberalism had sought to discard) and the policies needed to safeguard the nation, most notably protectionism and controls on migration.

The commitment to 'Make America Great Again' led to other promises. There was to be an industrial strategy based upon state action to resurrect the US's manufacturing base, an assertive trade policy and, as noted in other chapters, the protection of 'entitlements' for those deemed deserving.

In sum, whereas the early days of the financial crisis gave rise to claims that neoliberalism would be undermined by those on the Keynesian or Marxist left, it is instead being challenged by the populist right.

Thus, whereas neoliberalism survived the ghosts of Karl Marx and John Maynard Keynes, it is instead being laid low by a conflict-based form of politics that will progressively eradicate old solidarities and pit the 'people' against those who are not within its ranks. 'Trumpism' and European forms of populism are still in some ways weakly embedded but they may well exacerbate and intensify the battles and processes of group competition between different constituencies. Against this background, both the nation and state that neoliberalism sought to relegate to the sidelines will again take a place at the centre of the political stage. Alongside this, in place of the marketisation processes that were at the heart of neoliberalism, populist rule is often tied to a clientelistic form of politics based upon the buying off of core constituencies and the selective granting of favours through elite networks.

The possibility is thus opening up that the basis of the market order will take a very different and reconfigured or reordered form. Nigel Farage, at that point interim leader of UKIP, made the point in a rather sharper form. In an interview with CNN, he summed up the wave of changes during 2016 and highlighted the resurgence of the nation and state: 'What it's all about is – do you believe in nation-state democracy, or are you happy with bigger supra-national forms of government where decisions get taken elsewhere?' (quoted in Westcott, 2016).

In the face of this, there were some immediate signs that elites were swaying. Former Treasury Secretary Lawrence Summers, who had at times seemed to personify elite neoliberalism, appeared ready to abandon its founding principles by calling for a dialogue around 'responsible nationalism' and the adoption of measures that 'increase the range of policies that governments can pursue to support middle-class workers domestically' (quoted in Galston, 2016).

The populist project faces major obstacles. Because it is a set of sentiments rather than a coherent or structured ideology, populism is by definition unstable and often gives rise to parties and movements that prove short-lived. Furthermore, Marxists would argue that the logic of globalising markets and the structural power of the capitalist class will rein in Trump's commitment to the closing of borders and attempts to impose constraints upon firms' freedom of action. Put another way, 'establishment' Republicanism will win out. For their part, institutionalists emphasize the limits upon radical policy change that existing policy legacies and paths impose. Nonetheless, having said that, if facial expressions mean anything, the widely circulated photograph taken of Farage and Trump together in the wake of his election triumph showing the two men standing together and confidently beaming in a seemingly gold-plated lift at Trump Tower suggests that neoliberalism is likely to face a period of profound reordering, and prevailing institutional structures might well crack.

Notes

1   Having said this, Trump made some very visible 'outreach' efforts to African-American voters although commentators concluded that this was more a bid to head off claims that he was racist and thereby reassure suburban and largely college-educated whites.

References

Aberbach, Joel D. (2017) *Understanding Contemporary American Conservatism*, Abingdon: Routledge.

Anderson, Benedict (2016) *Imagined Communities: Reflections on the Origin and Spread of Nationalism*, London: Verso.

Ashbee, Edward (2000) 'The Politics of Paleoconservatism', *Society*, 37:3, March/April, 75–84.

Ashbee, Edward (2015) *The Right and the Recession*, Manchester: Manchester University Press.

Ashbee, Edward and John Dumbrell (2016) 'The Politics of Change', in Edward Ashbee and John Dumbrell (eds), *The Obama Presidency and the Politics of Change*, New York: Palgrave Macmillan, 1–50.

Ashbee, Edward and Alex Waddan (2010) 'The Obama Administration and United States Trade Policy', *Political Quarterly*, 81:2, April–June, 253–262.

Associated Press (2016) 'How Donald Trump's Plan to Ban Muslims Has Evolved', *Associated Press*, June 28th, http://fortune.com/2016/06/28/donald-trump-muslim-ban/. Accessed January 20th 2017.

Bai, Matt (2016) 'The Moment That Made Trump Possible', *Yahoo News*, December 15th, www.yahoo.com/news/the-moment-that-made-trump-possible-100008601.html. Accessed December 20th 2016.

Ban, Cornel (2016) 'Will Trump Bring Neoliberalism's Apocalypse, or Merely a New Iteration?', *Institute for New Economic Thinking*, November 30th, www.ineteconomics.org/perspectives/blog/will-trump-bring-neoliberalisms-apocalypse-or-merely-a-new-iteration. Accessed January 20th 2017.

REFERENCES

BBC News (2008) 'Marx Popular Amid Credit Crunch', *BBC News*, October 20th, http://news.bbc.co.uk/2/hi/europe/7679758.stm. Accessed November 28th 2016.

Beauchamp, Zack (2016) 'Donald Trump is uniquely American. But the forces behind his rise aren't', *Vox*, July 19th, www.vox.com/2016/7/19/12210652/donald-trump-european-right. Accessed December 2nd 2016.

Beckwith, Ryan Teague (2016) 'Read Donald Trump's Speech on the Orlando Shooting', *Time*, June 13th, http://time.com/4367120/orlando-shooting-donald-trump-transcript/. Accessed December 2nd 2016.

Berenson, Tessa and Sam Frizell (2016) 'Donald Trump, Hillary Clinton Warn of Doom in Dueling Speeches', *Time*, October 25th, http://time.com/4545517/donald-trump-hillary-clinton-florida-speeches/. Accessed November 10th 2016.

Berman, Russell (2016) 'What Bill Clinton Meant When He Called Obamacare "Crazy"', *The Atlantic*, October 4th, www.theatlantic.com/politics/archive/2016/10/bill-clinton-on-how-to-fix-crazy-obamacare/502868/. Accessed January 20th 2017.

Blow, Charles (2016a) 'Donald Trump Is Lying in Plain Sight', *The New York Times*, September 6th, www.nytimes.com/2016/09/08/opinion/donald-trump-is-lying-in-plain-sight.html?_r=0. Accessed October 27th 2016.

Blow, Charles M. (2016b) 'About the "Basket of Deplorables"', *The New York Times*, September 12th, www.nytimes.com/2016/09/12/opinion/about-the-basket-of-deplorables.html. Accessed October 14th 2016.

Borger, Julian (2016) 'World Leaders Brace Themselves For Trump Presidency', *The Guardian*, November 9th, www.theguardian.com/us-news/2016/nov/09/donald-trump-presidency-global-reactions-trade-deals. Accessed November 24th 2016.

Brennan Center for Justice (2016) *New Voting Restrictions in Place for 2016 Presidential Election*, www.brennancenter.org/voting-restrictions-first-time-2016. Accessed December 28th 2016.

Brewer, Mark D. (2016) 'Populism in American Politics', *The Forum*, 14:3, 249–264.

Brooks, David (2010) 'The Tea Party Teens', *The New York Times*, January 4th, www.nytimes.com/2010/01/05/opinion/05brooks.html?_r=0. Accessed January 20th 2017.

Bruce, Mary, Ben Siegel and John Parkinson (2016) 'House Speaker Paul Ryan Calls Trump's Win the Most "Incredible Political Feat" ', *ABC News*, November 9th, http://abcnews.go.com/Politics/house-speaker-paul-ryan-calls-trumps-win-incredible/story?id=43419719. Accessed January 20th 2017.

Buchanan, Patrick J. (2008) *Churchill, Hitler and 'The Unnecessary War'*, New York: Crown Publishers.

Bump, Philip (2016a) 'Donald Trump Took 5 Different Positions on Abortion in 3 Days', *The Fix (Washington Post)*, April 3rd, www.washingtonpost.com/news/the-fix/wp/2016/04/03/donald-trumps-ever-shifting-positions-on-abortion/. Accessed November 5th 2016.

Bump, Philip (2016b) 'Donald Trump Warns That 650 Million Immigrants Could Come to the U.S. in a Week. Let's Do The Math!', *Washington Post (The Fix)*, October 31st, www.washingtonpost.com/news/the-fix/wp/2016/10/31/donald-trump-warns-that-650-million-immigrants-could-come-to-the-u-s-in-a-week-lets-do-the-math/. Accessed November 30th 2016.

Bureau of Labor Statistics (2016) *Labor Force Statistics from the Current Population Survey*, Bureau of Labor Statistics, http://data.bls.gov/timeseries/LNS14000000. Accessed January 20th 2017.

Bycoffe, Aaron and David Wasserman (2016) 'What Would It Take To Turn Blue States Red?', *FiveThirtyEight*, October 5th, http://projects.fivethirtyeight.com/2016-swing-the-election/. Accessed January 20th 2017.

Caldwell, Leigh Ann and Benjy Sarlin (2016) 'Beyond Trump: Where Will the Republican Party Go After 2016?', *NBC News*, August 25th, www.nbcnews.com/specials/donald-trump-republican-party/gop-future. Accessed November 25th 2016.

Capano, Giliberto and Maria Tullia Galanti (2015) *Brokers, Entrepreneurs and Leaders in Policy Dynamics: From Individual Actors to Types of Agency*, Paper prepared for the 2nd International Conference in Public Policy, Milan, July 1st–4th.

Carnevale, Anthony P., Tamara Jayasundera and Artem Gulish (2016) *America's Divided Recovery: College Haves and Have-Nots*, Washington DC: Georgetown University Center on Education and the Workforce.

Carpenter, Daniel (2005) 'The Evolution of National Bureaucracy in the United States', in Joel Aberbach and Mark Peterson (eds), *The Executive Branch*, Oxford: Oxford University Press, 41–71.

Carson, Jamie L., Michael H. Crespin, Charles J. Finocchiaro and David W. Rohde (2007) 'Redistricting and Party Polarization in the U.S. House of Representatives', *American Politics Research*, 35:6, 878–904.

Carstensen, Martin B. (2011) 'Paradigm Man Vs. the Bricoleur: Bricolage as an Alternative Vision of Agency in Ideational Change', *European Political Science Review*, 3:1, 147–167.

Cassidy, John (2016) 'Why is Donald Trump in Michigan and Wisconsin?', *The New Yorker*, October 31st, www.newyorker.com/news/john-cassidy/why-is-donald-trump-in-michigan-and-wisconsin. Accessed January 12th 2017.

Charen, Mona (2016) 'Why Do They Hate Hillary Clinton?', *National Review*, June 30th, www.nationalreview.com/article/437345/hillary-clinton-lies-make-her-unpopular. Accessed October 14th 2016.

Chaturvedi, Richa (2016) 'A Closer Look at the Gender Gap in Presidential Voting', *Pew Research Center*, July 28th, www.pewresearch.org/fact-tank/2016/07/28/a-closer-look-at-the-gender-gap-in-presidential-voting/. Accessed October 19th 2016.

Chokshi, Niraj (2016) 'Trump Accuses Clinton of Guiding Global Elite Against U.S. Working Class', *The New York Times*, October 13th, www.nytimes.com/2016/10/14/us/politics/trump-comments-linked-to-antisemitism.html?_r=0. Accessed November 4th 2016.

Cillizza, Chris (2016) The 13 Most Amazing Findings in the 2016 Exit Poll', *The Washington Post*, November 10th, www.washingtonpost.com/news/the-fix/wp/2016/11/10/the-13-most-amazing-things-in-the-2016-exit-poll/?tid=pm_pop_b. Accessed December 27th 2016.

CNN Politics (2008) *Election Center – 2008: Exit Polls*, http://edition.cnn.com/ELECTION/2008/results/polls/#USP00p1. Accessed January 20th 2017.

CNN Politics (2016) 'Exit Polls', CNN Politics, November 9th, http://edition.cnn.com/election/results/exit-polls. Accessed January 20th 2017.

Cohen, Marty, David Karol, Hans Noel and John Zaller (2009) *The Party Decides: Presidential Nominations Before and After Reform*, Chicago: University of Chicago Press.

Collingwood, Loren (2016) 'The County-by-County Data on Trump Voters Shows Why He Won', *The Washington Post*, November 19th, www.washingtonpost.com/news/monkey-cage/wp/2016/11/19/the-country-by-county-data-on-trump-voters-shows-why-he-won/. Accessed December 8th 2016.

Corlett, Adam (2016) *Examining an Elephant: Globalisation and the Lower Middle Class of the Rich World*, The Resolution Foundation, www.resolutionfoundation.org/app/uploads/2016/09/Examining-an-elephant.pdf. Accessed January 2nd 2017.

Cox, Daniel and Robert P. Jones (2016) 'Still Live Near Your Hometown? If You're White, You're More Likely To Support Trump/PRRI/The Atlantic Survey', Public Religion Research Institute, October 6th, www.prri.org/research/prri-atlantic-oct-6-poll-politics-election-clinton-trump/. Accessed November 22nd 2016.

Cramer, Katherine J. (2016) *The Politics of Resentment: Rural Consciousness in Wisconsin and the Rise of Scott Walker*, Chicago: University of Chicago Press.

Davis, Mike (2016) 'Not a Revolution – Yet', *Verso*, November 15th, www.versobooks.com/blogs/2948-not-a-revolution-yet. Accessed January 10th 2017.

Devaney, Tim (2016) 'Study: Obama issued $743B in regs', *The Hill*, August 8th, http://thehill.com/regulation/290744-study-obama-issued-743b-in-regs. Accessed October 5th 2016.

Dobbs, Richard, Anu Madgavkar, James Manyika, Jonathan Woetzel, Jacques Bughin, Eric Labaye and Pranav Kashyap (2016) *Poorer Than Their Parents? A New Perspective On Income Inequality*, McKinsey Global Institute, www.mckinsey.com/global-themes/employment-and-growth/poorer-than-their-parents-a-new-perspective-on-income-inequality. Accessed January 20th 2017.

Dugan, Andrew (2013) 'On 10th Anniversary, 53% in U.S. See Iraq War as Mistake', *Gallup*, March 18th, www.gallup.com/poll/161399/

10th-anniversary-iraq-war-mistake.aspx. Accessed September 29th 2016.

Farhang, Sean (2010) *The Litigation State: Public Regulation and Private Lawsuits in the United States*, Princeton: Princeton University Press.

Fiorina, Morris P. with Samuel J. Abrams and Jeremy C. Pope (2005) *Culture War? The Myth of a Polarized America*, London: Pearson Longman.

Foster, Peter (2016) 'Viktor Orban Heralds Donald Trump's Win As Start Of Europe Counter-Revolution: "What A Day! The Era Of Liberal Non-Democracy Is Over"', *The Daily Telegraph*, November 11th, www.telegraph.co.uk/news/2016/11/11/viktor-orban-heralds-donald-trumps-win-as-start-of-europe-counte/. Accessed December 17th 2016.

Foucault, Michael (2010) *The Birth of Biopolitics: Lectures at the College de France*, London: Palgrave Macmillan.

Frank, Thomas (2005) *What's the Matter with Kansas?: How Conservatives Won the Heart of America*, New York: Holt Paperbacks.

Gallup (2016) *Trust in Government*, www.gallup.com/poll/5392/trust-government.aspx. Accessed March 28th 2017.

Galston, William A. (2016) 'The Year Populism Went Mainstream', *The Wall Street Journal*, December 6th, www.wsj.com/articles/the-year-populism-went-mainstream-1481070623. Accessed January 20th 2017.

Gardiner, Nile (2016) 'The Trump Revolution Will Reshape America For The Better In 2017', *The Daily Telegraph*, December 28th, www.telegraph.co.uk/news/2016/12/28/trump-revolution-will-reshape-america-better-2017/. Accessed January 7th 2017.

Golshan, Tara (2016) 'Jill Stein Voters Did Not Deliver Donald Trump the Presidency', *Vox*, November 11th, www.vox.com/policy-and-politics/2016/11/11/13576798/jill-stein-third-party-donald-trump-win. Accessed December 20th 2016.

Gottfried, Paul (2008) 'The Decline and Rise of the Alternative Right', *Taki's Magazine*, December 1st, http://takimag.com/article/the_decline_and_rise_of_the_alternative_right/print#ixzz4Seb0TmZi. Accessed December 21st 2016.

Gottfried, Paul (2016) 'Some Observations from the Man who created Alt-Right', *Frontpage Magazine*, August 30, www.frontpagemag.com/fpm/263988/some-observations-man-who-created-alt-right-paul-gottfried. Accessed March 24th 2017.

Greenberg, Stanley (2008) 'Goodbye, Reagan Democrats', *The New York Times*, November 10th, www.nytimes.com/2008/11/11/opinion/11greenberg.html?_r=2&ref=opinion&oref=slogin. Accessed January 12th 2017.

Hacker, Jacob S. (2004) 'Privatizing Risk without Privatizing the Welfare State: The Hidden Politics of Social Policy Retrenchment in the United States', *American Political Science Review*, 98:2, 243–260.

Hacker, Jacob S. and Paul Pierson (2005) *Off Center: The Republican Revolution and the Erosion of American Democracy*, New Haven and London: Yale University Press.

Hains, Tim (2016) 'Coulter: Trump Victory Boils Down to 'Globalism vs. Nationality'', *Real Clear Politics*, November 9th, www.realclearpolitics.com/video/2016/11/09/coulter_trump_victory_boils_down_to_globalism_vs_nationality.html. Accessed November 30th 2016.

Hall, Peter A. and Michele Lamont (2013) *Social Resilience in the Neoliberal Era*, Cambridge: Cambridge University Press.

Hamilton, Alexander (n.d.) *The Federalist Papers: No. 68*, Yale Law School, http://avalon.law.yale.edu/18th_century/fed68.asp. Accessed November 29th 2016.

Hay, Colin (2011) 'Ideas and the Construction Of Interests', in Daniel Béland and Robert Henry Cox (eds), *Ideas and Politics in Social Science Research*, Oxford: Oxford University Press, 65–82.

Heer, Jeet (2016) Trump's Lies Destroy Logic As Well As Truth', *The New Republic*, November 28th, https://newrepublic.com/article/139025/trumps-lies-destroy-logic-well-truth. Accessed December 23rd 2016.

Heilemann, John and Mark Halperin (2010) *Game Change: Obama and the Clintons, McCain and Palin, and the Race of a Lifetime*, New York: Harper Perrenial.

Heinö, Andreas Johansson (2016) *Timbro Authoritarian Populism Index*, Stockholm: Timbro.

Hohmann, James (2016) 'The Daily 202: Trump Over Performed the Most in Counties with the Highest Drug, Alcohol and Suicide

Mortality Rates', *The Washington Post*, December 9th, www.washingtonpost.com/news/powerpost/paloma/daily-202/2016/12/09/daily-202-trump-over-performed-the-most-in-counties-with-the-highest-drug-alcohol-and-suicide-mortality-rates/584a2a59e9b69b7e58e45f2e/?utm_term=.8746e1a04034. Accessed January 18th 2017.

Hofstadter, Richard (1996 [1963]) *The Paranoid Style in American Politics*, Cambridge, MA: Harvard University Press.

Hohmann, James (2016) 'The Daily 202: The Reagan Democrats are no longer Democrats. Will they ever be again?', *The Washington Post*, November 11th, www.washingtonpost.com/news/powerpost/paloma/daily-202/2016/11/11/daily-202-the-reagan-democrats-are-no-longer-democrats-will-they-ever-be-again/58252889e9b69b6085905df0/?utm_term=.71ca25be877d. Accessed March 27th 2017.

Howard, Christopher (1997) *The Hidden Welfare State: Tax Expenditures and Social Policy in the United States*, Princeton: Princeton Paperbacks.

Howard, Christopher (2007) *The Welfare State Nobody Knows: Debunking Myths about US Social Policy*, Princeton: Princeton University Press.

Huang, Jon, Samuel Jacoby, K.K. Rebecca Lai and Michael Strickland (2016) 'Election 2016: Exit Polls', *The New York Times*, November 8th, www.nytimes.com/interactive/2016/11/08/us/politics/election-exit-polls.html?_r=0. Accessed November 12th 2016.

Jacobs, Lawrence and Desmond King (eds) (2009) *The Unsustainable American State*, Oxford: Oxford University Press.

Jacques, Martin (2016) 'The Death of Neoliberalism and the Crisis in Western Politics', *The Guardian*, August 21st, www.theguardian.com/commentisfree/2016/aug/21/death-of-neoliberalism-crisis-in-western-politics. Accessed September 27th 2016.

Jeffrey, Terence P. (2016) 'U.S. Has Record 10th Straight Year Without 3% Growth in GDP', *CBS News*, February 26th, www.cnsnews.com/news/article/terence-p-jeffrey/. Accessed November 10th 2016.

Judis, John B. (2016) *The Populist Explosion: How the Great Recession Transformed American and European Politics*, New York: Columbia Global Reports.

Keith, Bruce E., David B. Magleby, Candice J. Nelson, Elizabeth Orr, Mark C. Westlye and Raymond E. Wolfinger (1992) *The Myth of the Independent Voter*, Oakland: University of California Press.

Kemp, Geoffrey (2004) 'Losing the Peace?', *The National Interest*, Summer, http://nationalinterest.org/article/losing-the-peace-965. Accessed September 29th 2016.

King, Desmond S. (2016) 'The American State and the Enduring Politics of Race', in Orfeo Fioretos, Tulia G. Falleti and Adam Sheingate (eds), *The Oxford Handbook of Historical Institutionalism*, Oxford: Oxford University Press, 293–309.

Klain, Ronald A. (2016) 'Trump's Big Infrastructure Plan? It's a Trap', *The Washington Post*, November 18th, www.washingtonpost.com/opinions/trumps-big-infrastructure-plan-its-a-trap/2016/11/18/5b1d109c-adae-11e6-8b45-f8e493f06fcd_story.html?utm_term=.2c9b614c1b26. Accessed January 12th 2017.

Kriesi, Hanspeter and Takis S. Pappas (2016) *European Populism in the Shadow of the Great Recession*, Colchester: European Consortium for Political Research.

Lakoff, George (2014) *Don't Think of an Elephant: Know Your Values and Frame the Debate*, White River Junction, VT: Chelsea Green Publishing.

Lane, Charles (2016) 'Trump Wants to Make America More Like Denmark', *The Washington Post*, March 2nd, www.washingtonpost.com/opinions/trump-wants-to-make-america-more-like-denmark/2016/03/02/6bfc935e-dfd9-11e5-8d98-4b3d9215ade1_story.html. Accessed September 21st 2016.

Lind, Michael (2016) 'Donald Trump, the Perfect Populist', *Politico Magazine*, March 9th, www.politico.com/magazine/story/2016/03/donald-trump-the-perfect-populist-213697. Accessed September 19th 2016.

Lombroso, Daniel and Yoni Appelbaum (2016) ' "Hail Trump!": White Nationalists Salute the President Elect', *The Atlantic*, November 21st, www.theatlantic.com/politics/archive/2016/11/richard-spencer-speech-npi/508379/. Accessed January 5th 2017.

Los Angeles Times (2016) 'Campaign 2016 Updates: Obama Tells Trump to "Stop Whining" and Start Campaigning', *Los Angeles*

Times, October 18th, www.latimes.com/nation/politics/trailguide/la-na-trailguide-updates-donald-trump-proposes-congressional-1476820631-htmlstory.html. Accessed December 11th 2016.

Lundeen, Andrew (2015) 'How Much Do People Pay in Taxes?', *Tax Foundation*, April 14th, http://taxfoundation.org/blog/how-much-do-people-pay-taxes. Accessed September 27th 2016.

MacWilliams, Matthew (2016) 'The One Weird Trait That Predicts Whether You're a Trump Supporter', *Politico Magazine*, January 17th, www.politico.com/magazine/story/2016/01/donald-trump-2016-authoritarian-213533. Accessed November 2nd 2016.

Mahler, Jonathan and Dirk Johnson (2016) 'Mike Pence's Journey: Catholic Democrat to Evangelical Republican', *The New York Times*, July 21st, A12.

Mahoney, James 'Path Dependence in Historical Sociology', *Theory and Society*, August 2000, 29:4, 507–548.

Mann, Thomas E. and Norman J. Ornstein (2012) *It's Even Worse Than It Looks: How the American Constitutional System Collided with the New Politics of Extremism*, New York: Basic Books.

Matthews, Dylan (2016) 'Taking Trump Voters' Concerns Seriously Means Listening to What They're Actually Saying', *Vox*, October 15th, www.vox.com/policy-and-politics/2016/10/15/13286498/donald-trump-voters-race-economic-anxiety. Accessed November 18th 2016.

McCain, Robert Stacy (2009) 'Tea Party Nation', *The American Spectator*, November 13th, http://spectator.org/archives/2009/11/13/tea-party-nation/print. Accessed September 21st 2016.

McQuarrie, Michael (2016) *Trump and the Revolt of the Rust Belt*, LSE – US Centre, http://blogs.lse.ac.uk/usappblog/2016/11/11/23174/. Accessed January 17th 2017.

Merrill, Peter R. (2007) *The Corporate Tax Conundrum*, London: PricewaterhouseCoopers LLP, www.pwc.com/us/en/washington-national-tax/assets/corporate_tax_conundrum.pdf. Accessed November 14th 2016.

Mettler, Suzanne (2010) 'Reconstituting the Submerged State: The Challenges of Social Policy Reform in the Obama Era', *Perspectives on Politics*, 8:3, September, 803–824.

Mettler, Suzanne (2011) *The Submerged State*, Chicago: University of Chicago Press.

Moore, Stephen (2016) 'Why Tax Rate Cuts Work', *The Washington Times*, May 15th, www.washingtontimes.com/news/2016/may/15/stephen-moore-why-tax-rate-cuts-work/#pagebreak. Accessed December 1st 2016.

Moser, Bob (2016) 'Trump's Vanishing Base', *The New Republic*, November 21st, https://newrepublic.com/article/138877/trumps-vanishing-base. Accessed January 10th 2017.

Motta, Matt (2016) 'Trumpism Is Just As Popular In Denmark As the United States', *The Washington Post (Monkey Cage)*, December 22nd, www.washingtonpost.com/news/monkey-cage/wp/2016/12/22/trumpism-is-just-as-popular-in-denmark-as-the-united-states/?utm_term=.4532a3553e4a. Accessed January 8th 2017.

Müller, Jan-Werner (2016) *What is Populism?* Philadelphia: University of Pennsylvania Press.

Murdock, Deroy (2016) 'Enacting Trump's "Contract with the American Voter" would revive a nation in decline', *National Review*, October 26th, www.nationalreview.com/article/441458/donald-trump-contract-american-voter-gettysburg-address. Accessed March 27th 2017.

Muro, Mark and Sifan Liu (2016) 'Why Trump's Factory Job Promises Won't Pan Out – In One Chart', *The Brookings Institution*, November 21st, www.brookings.edu/blog/the-avenue/2016/11/21/why-trumps-factory-job-promises-wont-pan-out-in-one-chart/. Accessed December 18th 2016.

Murray, Charles (2013) *Coming Apart: The State of White America, 1960–2010*, New York: Crown Forum.

National Public Radio (2016) 'Is Trump's Deal With Carrier A Form Of Crony Capitalism?', National Public Radio, December 2nd, www.npr.org/2016/12/02/504042185/is-trumps-deal-with-carrier-a-form-of-crony-capitalism. Accessed January 5th 2017.

National Review (2016) 'Against Trump'; *National Review*, February 15th, 14–16.

New York Times (2016) 'Donald Trump's Alt-Right Brain', *New York Times*, September 5th, www.nytimes.com/2016/09/06/opinion/

donald-trumps-alt-right-brain.html?_r=0. Accessed March 24th 2017.

New York Times / CBS News (2010) *National Survey of Tea Party Supporters*, New York Times / CBS News, April 5th–12th, http://documents.nytimes.com/new-york-timescbs-news-poll-national-survey-of-tea-party-supporters?ref=politics. Accessed September 27th 2016.

Nossiter, Adam (2016) 'After Trump Win, Parallel Path Is Seen for Marine Le Pen of France's Far Right', *The New York Times*, November 11th, www.nytimes.com/2016/11/12/world/europe/donald-trump-marine-le-pen.html?_r=0. Accessed December 2nd 2016.

Oliver, Eric and Thomas Wood (2016) 'A New Poll Shows 52% of Republicans Actually Think Trump Won The Popular Vote', *The Washington Post*, December 18th, www.washingtonpost.com/news/monkey-cage/wp/2016/12/18/a-new-poll-shows-an-astonishing-52-of-republicans-think-trump-won-the-popular-vote/?utm_term=.97b3682444b3. Accessed January 19th 2017.

Organisation for Economic Co-operation and Development (2016), *Income Distribution and Poverty: By Country*, Organisation for Economic Co-operation and Development, http://stats.oecd.org/index.aspx?queryid=66670. Accessed October 12th 2016.

Pacewicz, Josh (2016) 'Here's the Real Reason Rust Belt Cities and Towns Voted For Trump', *The Washington Post (Monkey Cage)*, December 20th, www.washingtonpost.com/news/monkey-cage/wp/2016/12/20/heres-the-real-reason-rust-belt-cities-and-towns-voted-for-trump/?utm_term=.f89ebfd14f3b&wpisrc=nl_cage&wpmm=1. Accessed January 14th 2017.

Patel, Jugal K. and Wilson Andrews (2016) 'Trump's Electoral College Victory Ranks 46th in 58 Elections', *The New York Times*, December 18th, www.nytimes.com/interactive/2016/12/18/us/elections/donald-trump-electoral-college-popular-vote.html?hp&action=click&pgtype=Homepage&clickSource=story-heading&module=first-column-region&region=top-news&WT.nav=top-news&_r=0. Accessed January 11th 2017.

Pew Research Center (2015a) *Beyond Distrust: How Americans View Their Government*, Pew Research Center, November 23rd, www.people-press.org/files/2015/11/11-23-2015-Governance-release.pdf. Accessed September 29th 2016.

Pew Research Center (2015b) 'Negative Views of Supreme Court at Record High, Driven by Republican Dissatisfaction', *Pew Research Center*, July 29th, www.people-press.org/2015/07/29/negative-views-of-supreme-court-at-record-high-driven-by-republican-dissatisfaction/. Accessed September 29th 2016.

Pew Research Center (2016a) *In Their Own Words: Why Voters Support – and Have Concerns About – Clinton and Trump*, Pew Research Center, September 21st, www.people-press.org/2016/09/21/in-their-own-words-why-voters-support-and-have-concerns-about-clinton-and-trump/. Accessed January 3rd 2017.

Pew Research Center (2016b) *Election 2016–5. Issues and the 2016 Campaign*, Pew Research Center, August 18th, www.people-press.org/2016/08/18/5-issues-and-the-2016-campaign/. Accessed November 11th 2016.

Piggott, Stephen (2016) 'Is Breitbart.com Becoming the Media Arm of the "Alt-Right"?', *Southern Poverty Law Center*, April 28th, www.splcenter.org/hatewatch/2016/04/28/breitbartcom-becoming-media-arm-alt-right. Accessed January 8th 2017.

Pollard, Michael and Joshua Mendelsohn (2016) 'RAND Kicks Off 2016 Presidential Election Panel Survey', *RAND Corporation*, www.rand.org/blog/2016/01/rand-kicks-off-2016-presidential-election-panel-survey.html. Accessed January 17th 2017.

Prasad, Monica (2006) *The Politics of Free Markets: The Rise of Neoliberal Economic Policies in Britain, France, Germany & the United States*, Chicago: University of Chicago Press.

Prasad, Monica and Yingying Deng (2009) 'Taxation and the Worlds of Welfare', *Socio-Economic Review*, July, 7:3, 431–457.

Prokop, Andrew (2016a) 'Trump Fanned a Conspiracy About Obama's Birthplace For Years. Now He Pretends Clinton Started It', *Vox*, September 16th, www.vox.com/2016/9/16/12938066/donald-trump-obama-birth-certificate-birther. Accessed December 18th 2016.

Prokop, Andrew (2016b) Trump Backers Hate "Political Correctness." That's Why Gaffes Don't Hurt Him', *Vox*, February 29th, www.vox.com/2016/2/29/11133796/donald-trump-political-correctness. Accessed January 15th 2017.

Public Policy Polling (2016) 'Clinton's Florida Lead Continues to Grow', *Public Policy Polling*, October 14th, www.publicpolicypolling.

com/pdf/2015/PPP_Release_FL_104161.pdf. Accessed December 1st 2016.

Rachman, Gideon (2016) 'Donald Trump, Vladimir Putin and the Lure of the Strongman', *The Financial Times*, May 16th, www.ft.com/content/1c6ff2ce-1939-11e6-b197-a4af20d5575e. Accessed January 14th 2017.

Rattner, Steven (2017) '2016 in Charts. (And Can Trump Deliver in 2017?)', *The New York Times*, January 3rd, www.nytimes.com/2017/01/03/opinion/2016-in-charts-and-can-trump-deliver-in-2017.html?_r=0. Accessed January 3rd 2017.

Roper Center for Public Opinion Research (2015) *If I Were a Rich Man: Public Attitudes About Wealth and Taxes*, Roper Center for Public Opinion Research (Cornell University), June 11th, https://ropercenter.cornell.edu/public-attitudes-wealth-taxes/. Accessed September 29th 2016.

Rorty, Richard (1998) *Achieving our Country: The William E. Massey Sr. Lectures in the History of American Civilization*, Cambridge, MA: Harvard University Press.

Rove, Karl (2013) 'Karl Rove: The GOP's Self-Defeating "Defunding' Strategy"', *The Wall Street Journal*, September 18th, http://online.wsj.com/news/articles/SB10001424127887324492604579082851832871952. Accessed September 15th 2016.

Rucker, Philip (2009) 'Sen. DeMint of S.C. Is Voice of Opposition to Health-Care Reform', *Washington Post*, July 28th, www.washingtonpost.com/wp-dyn/content/article/2009/07/27/AR2009072703066_2.html?sid=ST2009072703107. Accessed October 23rd 2016.

Sailer, Steve (2000) 'GOP Future Depends on Winning Larger Share of the White Vote', *VDARE*, November 28th, www.vdare.com/articles/gop-future-depends-on-winning-larger-share-of-the-white-vote. Accessed October 18th 2016.

Salvanto, Anthony (2016) 'Poll: Gender Gap in Views on Trump Tape Describing Advances on Women', *CBS News*, October 9th, www.cbsnews.com/news/poll-gender-gap-in-views-on-trumps-2005-tape/. Accessed December 16th 2016.

Sanchez, Gabriel and Matt A. Barreto (2016) 'In Record Numbers, Latinos Voted Overwhelmingly Against Trump. We Did the Research', *The Washington Post* (*The Monkey Cage*), November

11t**ʰ**, www.washingtonpost.com/news/monkey-cage/wp/2016/ 11/11/in-record-numbers-latinos-voted-overwhelmingly-against-trump-we-did-the-research/. Accessed January 10th 2017.

Sanneh, Kelefa (2017) 'Intellectuals for Trump', *The New Yorker*, January 9th, www.newyorker.com/magazine/2017/01/09/intellectuals-for-trump?currentPage=all. Accessed January 9th 2017.

Schumpeter, Joseph A. (1994 [1942]) *Capitalism, Socialism and Democracy*. London: Routledge.

Seabrooke, Leonard (2005) *Legitimacy Gaps and Everyday Institutional Change in Interwar British Economy*, Working Paper #14, Copenhagen: Copenhagen Business School International Center for Business and Politics.

Seabrooke, Leonard (2007) 'The Everyday Social Sources of Economic Crises: From "Great Frustrations" to "Great Revelations" in Interwar Britain', *International Studies Quarterly*, 51:4, December, 795–810.

Sevastopulo, Demetri (2016) 'US Election: The Rise of the Trump Democrats', *The Financial Times*, October 4th, www.ft.com/content/b6e5555c-8972-11e6-8cb7-e7ada1d123b1. Accessed March 28th 2017.

Silver, Nate (2015) 'Donald Trump's Six Stages of Doom', *FiveThirtyEight*, August 6th, http://fivethirtyeight.com/features/donald-trumps-six-stages-of-doom/. Accessed September 23rd 2016.

Skidelsky, Robert (2009) *Keynes: The Return of the Master*, New York: PublicAffairs.

Skocpol, Theda and Vanessa Williamson (2012) *The Tea Party and the Remaking of American Conservatism*, Oxford: Oxford University Press.

Starr, Paul and Gøsta Esping-Andersen (1979) 'Passive Intervention', *Working Papers for a New Society*, July/August, 15–23, www.princeton.edu/~starr/articles/articles68-79/Starr_Esping-Andersen_Passive_Intervention.pdf. Accessed October 2nd 2016.

Steinmo, Sven (1989) 'Political Institutions and Tax Policy in the United States, Sweden, and Britain', *World Politics*, 41:4, July, 500–535.

Tax Foundation (2009) *OECD Nations Continue Cutting Corporate Tax Rates While U.S. Stands Still (Federal Plus Provincial/State*

Corporate Tax Rates for OECD Countries, 2008–2009), August 3rd, www.taxfoundation.org/taxdata/show/23473.html. Accessed October 21st 2016.

Tesler, Michael (2016) 'Views About Race Mattered More in Electing Trump Than in Electing Obama', *The Washington Post*, November 22nd, www.washingtonpost.com/news/monkey-cage/wp/2016/11/22/peoples-views-about-race-mattered-more-in-electing-trump-than-in-electing-obama/?tid=hybrid_collaborative_1_na. Accessed January 2nd 2017.

Tufekci, Zeynep (2016) 'Adventures in the Trump Twittersphere', *New York Times*, March 31st, www.nytimes.com/2016/03/31/opinion/campaign-stops/adventures-in-the-trump-twittersphere.html?_r=0. Accessed November 13th 2016.

US Census Bureau (2016) *Income and Poverty in the United States: 2015*, www.census.gov/topics/income-poverty/income.html. Accessed November 4th 2016.

Vacano, Diego Von (2016) 'Opinion: Trump Embraces Caudillo Politics as Latin America Shuns It', *NBC News*, November 22nd, www.nbcnews.com/news/latino/opinion-trump-embraces-caudillo-politics-latin-america-shuns-it-n686861. Accessed January 9th 2017.

Vogel, David (1986) *National Styles of Regulation: Environmental Policy in Great Britain and the United States*, Ithaca and London: Cornell University Press.

Wallace, Gregory and Robert Yoon (2016) 'Voter Turnout At 20-Year Low In 2016', CNN Politics, November 12th, http://edition.cnn.com/2016/11/11/politics/popular-vote-turnout–2016/. Accessed January 2nd 2017.

Warzel, Charlie and Lam Thuy Vo (2016) 'Here's Where Donald Trump Gets His News', *BuzzFeed News*, December 3rd, www.buzzfeed.com/charliewarzel/trumps-information-universe?utm_term=.ctN27ydllG#.hl4En5appx. Accessed January 3rd 2017.

Washington Post (2015) 'Full Text: Donald Trump Announces A Presidential Bid' *Washington Post*, June 16th, www.washingtonpost.com/news/post-politics/wp/2015/06/16/full-text-donald-trump-announces-a-presidential-bid/. Accessed January 20th 2017.

Watts, Simon, Allyson Holbrook and Maxwell Smith (2015) 'Policy Entrepreneurs and the Role of Advanced Cognition in Policy

Innovation', *Australian Journal of Business and Economic Studies*, 1:1, March, 18–27.

Westcott, Ben (2016) 'Brexit Leader Nigel Farage Calls Obama a Loathsome Creature', CNN Politics, November 11th, http://edition.cnn.com/2016/11/11/politics/nigel-farage-donald-trump-radio/. Accessed January 13th 2017.

Widmaier, Wesley, Mark Blyth and Leonard Seabrooke (2007) 'Exogenous Shocks or Endogenous Constructions?: The Meanings of Wars and Crises', *International Studies Quarterly*, 51:4, 747–759.

Williams, Jennifer (2016) 'Trump Is Spending The Last Days Before the Election Pandering to Conspiracy Theorists', *Vox*, November 5th, www.vox.com/presidential-election/2016/11/5/13534192/trump-ad-new-world-order-conspiracy-theory-neo-nazis. Accessed November 9th 2016.

Williams, Joan C. (2016) 'What So Many People Don't Get About the U.S. Working Class', *Harvard Business Review*, November 10th, https://hbr.org/2016/11/what-so-many-people-dont-get-about-the-u-s-working-class. Accessed January 7th 2017.

Williamson, John (2004) *A Short History of the Washington Consensus*, Washington DC: Peterson Institute for International Economics, https://piie.com/publications/papers/williamson0904-2.pdf. Accessed November 3rd 2016.

Worstall, Tim (2016) 'No Matter What Trump Says, Coal Mining Jobs Are Not Returning To West Virginia', *Forbes*, May 5th, www.forbes.com/sites/timworstall/2016/05/05/like-manufacturing-jobs-to-china-whatever-trump-says-mining-jobs-are-not-returning-to-w-virginia/#772d5c4d6f48. Accessed January 7th 2017.

Zito, Salena (2016) 'Taking Trump Seriously, Not Literally', *The Atlantic*, September 23rd, www.theatlantic.com/politics/archive/2016/09/trump-makes-his-case-in-pittsburgh/501335/. Accessed December 12th 2016.

Index

advocacy 26, 82
Affordable Childcare and Eldercare Act 15, 17–19, 56, 83
agencies 10, 12–13
Alt-right 4, 47, 50–52, 60, 85
America First 41, 55
American Energy and Infrastructure Act 56
American Recovery and Reinvestment Act (2009) 17
amnesty 29
Articles of Confederation (1781) 49
authoritarianism 44–45

Bachmann, Michele 2
Baghdad 27
Belgium 73
Berlusconi, Silvio 40, 46
'big government' 24, 27, 39, 67, 77, 83
Birtherism 34–35
blocs 5, 78
Brexit 1, 32
bricolage 52–53
Buchanan, Patrick J. 8, 50, 60, 85–87
Buckley, William F. 50

bureaucracy 17, 19
Bush, George H.W. 25, 50, 86
Bush, George W. 16, 25, 29, 48, 70, 83–84
Bush, Jeb 3

Cain, Herman 2
Cameron, David 90
candidate 3–4, 7, 24, 34, 43, 63, 67, 73, 80, 82, 87
capitalism 40, 47, 49
caudillismo 43–44
Clean up Corruption in Washington Act 57
Clinton, Bill 15, 25, 66
Clinton, Hillary 4, 7, 22–23, 33–35, 39, 42–43, 45, 61, 63, 65, 76, 80, 86
communism 8
Congress 1, 3, 12, 13, 16–18, 21, 25, 40, 56, 81, 87
conservatism 24–30, 47–54, 60, 74, 86, 91
conspiracy 31, 34–35, 77
Constitution (1787) 7, 18, 42, 48–49
Contract with America (1994) 56

corruption 31
cosmopolitanism 8
Coulter, Ann 33
counter-revolution 71
crisis 5, 13, 37, 58, 66, 88–93
'crony capitalism' 40
Cruz, Ted 3, 34, 86
culture 4–5, 9, 10, 29–30, 37, 47, 49, 51, 71

Declaration of Independence (1776) 26, 48
Democratic Party 9, 29, 39, 68–70
Denmark vi, 9, 39
deregulation 26, 88

economy 11, 67, 72, 86, 90
election 1, 4–7, 15–16, 19, 22, 24, 29–30, 33, 35, 41, 43–44, 48, 50, 52–54, 56, 58, 61–63, 65–67, 70–71, 74–79, 82–84, 87–88, 92, 95
Electoral College 1–2, 7, 23, 64
'emergency Keynesianism' 90
End the Offshoring Act 57
Erdogan, Recep Tayyip 44
ethnicity 32, 42, 47–48, 58, 62
Europe 6, 14–15, 31–32, 38–39, 46, 60, 71–73, 88, 90–92
exceptionalism 6
expenditure 12, 19

Fannie Mae (Federal National Mortgage Association) 11
Farage, Nigel 71, 94
Federal Reserve 90
finance capital 35, 59
Fiorina, Carly 86

fiscal policy 90
folkways 33, 47–48
Foucault, Michel 89–90
France 9, 11, 20
Frank, Thomas 29–30
Frankfurt 37
Freddie Mac (Federal Home Loan Mortgage Corporation) 11

GDP (Gross Domestic Product) 20, 24, 66
Germany 20, 50
Gettysburg 54, 56
Gini coefficient 90
globalisation 71–72
globalism 4, 33, 35, 59
Goldman Sachs 33
Gross Domestic Product *see* GDP

healthcare 5, 12, 14, 77
Heritage Foundation 1, 26
Hispanics 60, 68, 78
Hitler, Adolf 60
Homeowners Affordability and Stability Plan (2009) 17
Howard, Christopher 10
Huckabee, Mike 30
Hussein, Saddam 27

ideas 5, 8, 22, 24, 28, 36–37, 46–48, 50–54, 56, 58–59, 61, 82
identitarianism 51
illiberalism 6, 45
immigration 8–9, 21–22, 32, 35, 38, 48, 50, 57, 68, 71, 86
Immigration and Customs Enforcement 36

individualism 9
inflation 25, 66
institutionalisation 25
Internal Revenue Service 13
interventionism 12, 68
Iowa 65
Iraq 27–28, 58–59
ISIS 41
Islam 9, 38
Israel 41, 50

Johnson, Gary 87
Judis, John B. 18, 27, 31, 60, 83
jurisprudence 24, 56

Kasich, John 3
Kenya 34

Latinos 67
Le Pen, Marine 71
legitimacy 15, 19, 34, 36–37, 43, 83
liberalisation 26, 33, 40, 57, 67, 88
Lincoln, Abraham 54
lobbyists 19, 42, 57
Long, Huey 45

Marxism 90
McCain, John 3, 18, 29–30, 83
McKinsey & Company 11
Medicaid 15, 39, 56
Medicare 12, 15, 18, 39
Mettler, Suzanne 10
Mexico 36, 40–41
Michigan 18, 64–66
Middle Class Tax Relief and Simplification Act 54
monocausality 9

National Review 22, 24, 50
nationalism 8, 21, 33, 41, 44, 49, 51, 57, 71, 94
NBC 83
neoliberalism v, 1, 6, 26, 88, 90–91, 93–95
Nixon, Richard M. 24

Obama, Barack 8, 16–18, 34–35, 42–43, 53, 55, 59, 66, 68, 70–71, 77, 83, 85
Obamacare *see* Patient Protection and Affordable Care Act (2010)

paleo-conservatism 47, 49–52, 60, 86
Patient Protection and Affordable Care Act (2010) 15, 17–18, 56, 83–84
Pence, Mike 53, 60
Pennsylvania 24, 30, 65, 70, 93
Perot, Ross 21, 29
polarisation 5, 81–82
policy drift 25
populism 9–10, 22, 31–35, 38–39, 44–47, 52, 54, 57, 71, 91–94
Poujadisme 9
presidency 2–3, 6–7, 17, 24, 34, 49, 54–55, 64–65, 70, 77, 86
presidential election 7, 15, 19, 21, 33, 48, 63, 70, 76–77, 87–88
privatisation 39, 88
progressivism 38

quantitative easing 90

race 19, 32, 42, 48, 62, 75, 78–79, 89, 92
radicalism 18
reactive sequences 5, 7, 80–81
Reagan, Ronald 24–26, 29, 42, 52, 66
realignment 5, 28, 70
Realism 41, 50
reforms 17, 19, 24–25, 57, 66, 91
regulation 16, 24, 27, 53, 56, 77
Republicans 1, 3, 12, 16–17, 19, 24, 27, 29–30, 41, 43, 53, 56–58, 63–64, 70–71, 75–76, 83–84, 90
retrenchment 25
Romney, Mitt 3, 29–30, 43, 57, 65, 83
Roosevelt, Franklin D. 28, 49
Rubio, Marco 3
Russia 41
Ryan, Paul 2, 39, 55

Santorum, Rick 30
Scalia, Antonin 34, 56
Scandinavia 12
School Choice And Education Opportunity Act 55
Seabrooke, Leonard 36
Senate 17, 77, 83–84
Silver, Nate 2
Sisi, Abdel Fattah 44

Skocpol, Theda 74, 85
Social Security 11–12, 15, 39–40
sorting 82
sovereignty 21, 35–36
submerged state 10, 12

tax 10, 12–15, 17, 19–21, 25–28, 54–56, 60, 88
tax rate 14, 20, 88
tax revenue 20
Tea Party movement 3, 8, 18, 34, 39, 56, 66, 74, 83–85
terrorism 27
Turkey 44
Turner, Frederick Jackson 9
Twitter 37

United Kingdom 20–21, 32, 36, 90–91
universalism 14

value reinforcement 82
voting 5, 35, 63, 72, 74–75, 78

Wallace, George C. 8, 45, 63
war 8, 27, 29, 36, 50, 58–59, 85, 88
welfare 11, 14, 25, 28, 39
Wilders, Geert 71
Wisconsin 64, 65

EU authorised representative for GPSR:
Easy Access System Europe, Mustamäe tee 50,
10621 Tallinn, Estonia
gpsr.requests@easproject.com

www.ingramcontent.com/pod-product-compliance
Ingram Content Group UK Ltd.
Pitfield, Milton Keynes, MK11 3LW, UK
UKHW051122220326
48791PUK00013B/83